The British Disease

*A short essay on the nature and causes
of the nation's lagging wealth*

G. C. ALLEN

*Emeritus Professor of Political Economy,
University of London*

SECOND EDITION

Published by
THE INSTITUTE OF ECONOMIC AFFAIRS
1979

First published May 1976
Second Edition May 1979
©
THE INSTITUTE OF ECONOMIC AFFAIRS *1976, 1979*

ISSN 0073-2818

ISBN 0-255 36120-3

Printed in Great Britain by
The Garden City Press Limited
Letchworth, Hertfordshire SG6 1JS
Set in Intertype Baskerville

'The house of delusion is cheap to build but draughty to live in.'

A. E. HOUSMAN

CONTENTS

		Page
PREFACE	*Arthur Seldon*	9
PREFACE TO THE SECOND EDITION	*Arthur Seldon*	11
THE AUTHOR		14

I DECLINE AND FALL — 15

Causes of dissatisfaction with Britain's relative decline — 15
The cul de sac of 'demand management' — 16
American economists' criticism of British economy — 17
British economists neglect the fundamentals — 18
The fundamental questions — 19

II GOVERNMENT POLICY, BUREAUCRACY AND INDUSTRY — 20

Inadequacy of investment? A (qualified) red herring — 21
Management efficiency and worker attitudes — 21
Politicians and civil servants — 23
The quality of economic decision-makers is crucial, especially for innovation — 24
British economic policies have obstructed adaptation to change — 26
Government and public attitudes to leadership in industry — 27
Bureaucratic involvement has worsened relations between industry and government — 28
Influence of opinion-makers — 30

III GENESIS OF DECLINE IN 19TH CENTURY — 30

Early weakening of Britain's industrial lead — 30
Failure to take the lead in new industries — 32
Complacency by descendants of pioneers — 34
Disdain for trade — 35
Anti-manufacturing snobbery — 36
Strengths and faults of public schools *vis-à-vis* industry — 37
Failure of the universities to supply industrial leaders — 39
Vocational training in Continental universities — 41
The cult of the amateur — 42
Neglect of technical education: alarm in 1867 — 43
Britain lagged behind in business education — 45
Business education in Germany . . . — 46
. . . and in Japan — 47

[5]

Neglect of professional training to promote innovation   47
Role of the technical expert   49

IV   LATE ADAPTATION TO CHANGE   50
Tardy spread of professionalism in management   51
The West Midlands: lessons unheeded   52
Government policies frustrated adaptation to change   53
Industry's slow acceptance of post-war anti-
monopoly policy   54

V   THE PRESENT DAY: BRITAIN STILL LAGGING   55
British industry still failing to attract graduates and
professionals   55
Persisting cult of the amateur   56
The politician's nostalgia   57
The civil servants' shortcomings   57
'Planning': the fallacious comparison with France
and Japan   58
Government ignorance of conditions for industrial
efficiency   61
The 'British Disease' worsened by industrial rela-
tions   61
Industrial harmony foiled by craft unions   62
Trade unions more damaging in Britain than in
other countries   63
Marx, Galbraith, Schumpeter and capitalist conflict   64
Why more conflict in Britain than in other coun-
tries?   65
Management's attitude to industrial relations   66
Class divisions dramatised   67
Contrast with Japanese education and social atti-
tudes   68
British reluctance to learn from others   69

VI   THE SOLUTION: DEEP-SEATED ADAPTATION TO INDUS-
TRIAL SOCIETY   71
Resistance to change compounded by social structure   71
'Old ways and men of the old type'   72
Recovery long and painful: a change in values and
institutions   72

[6]

VII   THE WAY FORWARD   72
    1. Reward the successful   73
    2. Stop subsidies to the unsuccessful   73
    3. Higher priority for economic growth to support
       other aims   73
    4. Relate privileges and rewards to achievements,
       not status   74
    5. Raise standards of state primary schools to
       improve opportunities for intellect and character   74
    6. More civil servants should be educated in
       science and technology   75
    7. There should be a retreat from economic central-
       isation and new rules for operating the public
       sector   75
    8. More professional training for management
       necessary   75
    9. More attention to industrial relations by man-
       agements   76
   10. Leave scope for diversity in industrial organi-   76
       sation
POSTSCRIPT : *Britain on the Wrong Economic Road*   77
     Olson's 'stage of development' explanation   77
     The deficiencies of the British educational system   79
     The depreciation of science and technology   81
     The errors of government intervention   82
     The failure of government enterprise   84
     The hamstringing of management   86

Table 1. Comparative Economic Performance :
     1973 and 1977   78
QUESTIONS FOR DISCUSSION   89
NOTE ON READING   91

PREFACE

The *Hobart Papers* are intended to contribute authoritative, independent and lucid ' analyses to the understanding of the application of economic thinking to private and governmental activity. Their characteristic concern has been the optimum use of scarce resources and the extent to which it can be better achieved in markets using competitive pricing or by government using regulation based on centralised information and decision.

Professor G. C. Allen's *Hobart Paper* is a wide-ranging discussion of the origins of Britain's lagging economic progress. He argues it is necessary to go beyond the discussion of monetary management, the magnitude of government spending, or the amount of investment to the deep-seated attitudes to industry and the institutions of education and training to find the causes. He thus begins further back than the debate between the Keynesians and the Friedmanites over the role of money, or between the monetarists and the Hayekians over the 'cause' of inflation, to the discussions of the economists in the half century before the First World War such as W. J. Ashley, W. S. Jevons and Alfred Marshall on the development of industry in Britain and its performance compared to industry in North America and Europe. And he thus reinstates the grand tradition of political economy and asks searching and disturbing questions about the nature of society most conducive to economic advance and the weaknesses he discerns in 19th-century British society to which can be traced the origins of what has been called the 'British Disease'.

Professor Allen argues that the fundamental questions are whether the British people have been ready to accept the exertions required in a changing economy, whether the economically progressive countries have not been those that have concentrated on growth, whether Britain's social attitudes and economic institutions chime with modern industrialism, whether the low *quality* of investment, governmental and private (as distinct from its *quantity*), indicates weaknesses in the selection and training of civil servants and business managers, and why British industrial relations have become anachronistic to the point of attracting scorn from those who once regarded Britain as their exemplar. It is in the answers to these questions that he suggests the causes lie.

To supply the answers he goes back half a century and traces the deficiencies to their sources in the tardy development of education in science and technology and the reluctance of industry to use engineers and scientists. He goes further back to the industrial revolution and to the influence of the public schools and universities, especially Oxford and Cambridge, which in their pre-occupation with classical studies neglected education in the industrial arts; they excelled in providing administrators for government and the Empire but not for manufacturing and commerce. He argues that the civil servants and politicians produced by these institutions were not much interested in industry and did not understand the necessity for systematic training of professional scientists and engineers. Hence the relatively slow pace of adaptation to change compared to the USA, Germany, France and, in recent years, Japan, where there has been more respect for the entrepreneur and where industry values the scientist and has capitalised on technology.

Professor Allen's contention is thus that the main cause of the relative decline in British industry lies in the failure of attitudes and institutions to adapt themselves to a technological-industrial society. The British 'cult of the amateur' was inherited from an aristocratic society by its bourgeois successors. The increasing reluctance to accept an hierarchical society means that attitudes and institutions must be changed—gradually to avoid disorder but not too slowly if the British economy is to regain its initiatives. Old methods and leaders of the old type continued in Britain long after their counterparts had been replaced in other countries. In Britain the effort has been concentrated not on change but on conserving the industrial structure, and here the trade unions have strengthened the resistance to adaptation and innovation.

This *Hobart Paper* raises many fundamental issues on which economists and others will differ. Perhaps the most basic is whether the main fault lies with people and institutions that put continuity before innovation; or with government that by omission or commission failed to make the economy competitive so that people and institutions would have been impelled to adapt themselves to change; or even more fundamentally with the ideas and teachings of the critics of industrialism among historians and social observers who for a century or more have denigrated the role of risk-taking and investment in industry on the ground that the problems of production have been solved, to egalitarians who have fastened on redistribution as the means of raising the living standards of the 'under-privileged', and to those who have taught that work in profit-making industry is necessarily less worthy than work in salaried government, the professions, or teaching itself. Some blame may also be attached to representative machinery in government, industry and the trade unions that may not accurately represent the opinions and preferences of the rank and file, so that the voice of those who welcome change was muffled by that of others who preferred to settle for a quiet life. And the role of the state in controlling a large part of economic activity, from transport to education, and from fuel to medical care and housing, is not sacrosanct : in practice political power is not necessarily all-wise and far-sighted but prone to put short-term electoral expediency before long-term objectives.

The Institute wishes to thank Professors Margaret Gowing, Harold Rose and B. S. Yamey for reading an early draft and offering comments that the author has borne in mind in his final revisions. Since the *Paper* touches on the structure of industry and the attitude of industrialists, Sir Emmanuel Kaye, Chairman of Lansing Bagnall, Mr Kenneth Corfield, Managing Director of Standard Telephones and Cables, and Dr John Murray, Chairman of Bondworth Holdings, were also asked to offer observations on the general theme based on their knowledge and experience.

The constitution of the Institute requires it to dissociate its Trustees, Directors and Advisers from the analysis and conclusions of its authors, but it publishes this *Hobart Paper* as a scholarly, readable and thoughtful analysis of the far-reaching reasons for Britain's disappointing economic performance that will be found stimulating by students and teachers of economics, by people in government and industry, and, not least, by all who have been critical of British industry.

March 1976   ARTHUR SELDON

PREFACE TO THE SECOND EDITION

Perhaps the most important observation by Professor Allen in his Postscript to the Second Edition is that, although his argument has been widely accepted, nothing has been done about it. He is one among many economists who feel that, although the nation's leaders have had to accept the analysis of liberal economists on the causes of Britain's ills—not only the slow rate

[11]

of growth but also inflation, unemployment, the deteriorating 'public' services, not least, education and medicine, the growing social tensions and industrial conflicts—they have shown themselves unable to apply the only solutions that seem likely to remove the causes. Professor Allen says that, in the nearly three years since the First Edition, complacency has changed to a mood of humility, but there is still little sense of urgency that time is running out. There is still too little recognition that living standards derive from individual effort, exertion and enterprise, and that the vast mass of government expenditure requires taxation that is inimical to all three. There is too little acceptance that government expenditure will have· to be reduced by measures more radical than have been considered so far.

Professor Allen contests the view of the American Professor Mancur Olson that 'the British disease' is common to other countries at a given stage in industrial development. He insists that it is a *British* disease. To adapt Shakespeare (*via* Cassius):

'The fault, dear Britons, is not in our stars,
But in ourselves, that we are underlings'.

Professor Allen argues that 'a nation's future is settled by its choices'. Government has used its powers to strengthen the collective activities and collective demands that go against the grain of the market economy; Britain would by now not be lagging behind other countries (Table 1 of the Postcript) if government had gone with the grain of the market. Perhaps she would lag less if the disease proved infectious in Germany (and Australia, where trade unions are becoming obstructive of change); but that would hardly help mankind.

There are here lessons for Britain in 1979 and the 1980s. Indirectly, of course, industry is financing education by channelling its financial treasure through government. It thereby subjects the process to the pressures of party politics and of electoral calculations. It has thus acquiesced in the process by which short-term party politics has replaced the long-term industrial considerations that would have been given primacy in the judgements, decisions and policies on the role of science in industry. The notion that government would take a longer and wider view than would industry has never been persuasive, and never less than in our day when we have seen how government has used its influence in the investment decisions of the nationalised industries and public corporations. There is no reason to suppose it will ever be different.

The one argument that seems to have some weight is that the family influence in British industry has been a weakness because the sons of entrepreneurial fathers have not always inherited their talents, but have been content to rest on their oars and have thus neglected the contribution of science and technology. But it has little relevance for public policy. First, relative complacency would have been short-lived if the economy had been more competitive. Secondly, the alternative of political influence in industry would have been, and has been shown to have been, even more weakening, because it is more difficult to discipline complacent politicians than the complacent sons of innovating industrialists.

This is the reply to the critics of British management, including the heir to the throne, which would have had to be more cost-conscious, more efficient, better at 'communicating' with its work-force if it had been so impelled by the pressures of a more competitive system. That the British economy has not been more competitive is the responsibility of government, not of management.

Professor Allen has written his Postscript in beautiful classical English, uncluttered by jargon or sociologese, that is a lesson to younger economists. The Second Edition of his *Hobart Paper* is a timely addition to the literature on the economics (and social and political history) of Britain's present discontents that will require early and perhaps unprecedentedly drastic solutions.

March 1979   ARTHUR SELDON

THE AUTHOR

G. C. ALLEN is Emeritus Professor of Political Economy, University of London. Born in 1900 and educated at King Henry VIII School, Coventry, and the University of Birmingham, where he was a Research Fellow and Lecturer, 1925–29; Lecturer in Economics at the Higher Commercial College, Nagoya, Japan, 1922–25; Professor of Economics and Commerce, University College, Hull, 1929–33; Brunner Professor of Economic Science, University of Liverpool, 1933–47; and finally Professor of Political Economy, University College London, 1947–67. He was President of the Economics Section, British Association, in 1950; a member of the Monopolies Commission, 1950 to 1962. Author of books on industrial and economic development, including *Monopoly and Restrictive Practices* (1968) and *Japan's Economic Expansion* (1965). He has also written two well-known textbooks on the structure of British industry: *British Industries and their Organisation* (1933, revised edn. 1970), and *The Structure of Industry in Britain* (1961, revised edn. 1970).

For the IEA, of which he is a Trustee, Professor Allen has written *Economic Fact and Fantasy* (Occasional Paper 14, 1967, 2nd edn. 1969), an essay, 'Competition and Mergers', in *Mergers, Take-overs and the Structure of Industry* (IEA Readings No. 10, 1973), Part II of *The Price of Prosperity: Lessons from Japan* (Hobart Paper 58, 1974), and *How Japan Competes: A Verdict on 'Dumping'* (Hobart Paper 81, 1978).

I. DECLINE AND FALL

Long before Britain was engulfed by the great inflation, her people had become profoundly dissatisfied with her economic performance and foreigners spoke with dismay or *schadenfreude* of the 'English disease'. Yet it is paradoxical that the spread of this dissatisfaction should have occurred during a period in which Britain could claim to have done well in comparison with her immediate past.

All the statistical measures (when every allowance has been made for their imperfections) show that during the 1950s and 1960s her rate of economic growth was far higher than in any decade within the previous half-century. Between 1920 and 1937 the gross domestic product (at factor cost) increased by just over a third; in the 20 years between 1950 and 1970 it increased by nearly two-thirds. Output (GDP) per man-year was stationary between the beginning of the century and the outbreak of the First World War, and rose by only one-fifth by 1938; it increased by over a half between 1950 and 1970. Manufacturing industry taken alone showed similar comparisons. The output of manufactured goods doubled between 1900 and 1938; in the 20 years after 1950 it rose by just about as much. These advances in production were, of course, reflected in equivalent improvements in the standard of living. Even the British export performance, so often a target for criticism, was better in the two post-war decades than in the previous 50 years. The quantum of exports in 1938 was almost exactly the same as in 1900 whereas between 1950 and 1970 it nearly trebled.[1]

Causes of dissatisfaction with Britain's relative decline

Why then the widespread dissatisfaction with Britain's economic achievements? There are two reasons. First, although the comparatively high growth rate brought about a substantial rise in the standard of living for the mass of the population, it was still not fast enough to meet the expectations awakened by the large promises of politicians and stimulated by the 'demonstration effect' produced by rapid developments in communications and the arts of publicity. Secondly, Britain's performance in the post-

---

[1] Figures taken from *The British Economy; Key Statistics, 1909–1970*, published for the London and Cambridge Economic Service by Times Newspapers. The figures for growth are in real terms.

war period, despite its good showing compared with earlier years, was inferior to that of several other advanced countries.[2] The members of the OECD, including Japan, nearly trebled their industrial production between 1950 and 1970, whereas Britain's industrial production as a whole (not merely manufacturing) rose by less than three-quarters. It is true that in 1950 several of the chief industrial countries were still in the early stages of recovery from the devastation of the war. What is disquieting about Britain's performance is that, after the recovery stage had passed in Europe and Japan, her comparative rate of growth remained unfavourable. During the 1960s industrial production in the OECD countries as a whole grew more than twice as fast as in Britain, and after 1970 the disparity widened.

The consequence was that by the early 1970s income per head in Britain had fallen well below that of all other members of the EEC, except Italy. The British had long reconciled themselves to being poorer than the people of the United States, Canada and Sweden (as measured in income per head). Now they found themselves outpaced also by the West Germans, French, Belgians, Dutch, Norwegians, Danes, Swiss, Australians and Japanese. And the gap between Britain and several other countries, previously unremarked as serious rivals, was narrowing year by year. Although Britain's exports had shared in the expansion of world trade in the post-war era, her proportion of the aggregate manufactured exports fell from 25 per cent in 1950 to 11 per cent in 1970.[3] All this occurred before the British Treasury had lost control over public expenditure and brought the country to the verge of a hyper-inflation. By 1974 Britain's exports had fallen to under 9 per cent of the total.

The cul de sac of 'demand management'

The causes of this relative economic decline have been debated for many years among some of the most distinguished economists. The list of factors held to be responsible for the 'English sickness' (now re-named 'the British disease') has now become familiar, even though contributors to the discussion have found ample scope for disagreement about their importance. Many economists

---

[2] It might be argued that it would have been very surprising indeed if Britain had *not* done better in a period of rapidly advancing world technology, and of rapidly expanding international trade, than in a period of heavy chronic unemployment and stagnant international trade.
[3] It was, of course, inevitable that Britain's share should decline as the countries whose trade had been destroyed, or seriously damaged, by the war returned to world markets.

[16]

have emphasised defects in the management of demand. The neo-Keynesians have contended that the trouble has arisen from the refusal of the government to maintain a consistently high pressure of effective demand. Their opponents believe that an obsession with 'full employment' has been the source of the malaise. The neo-Keynesians point to the mischievous effects of 'stop-and-go' policies on industrial enterprise and investment. Non-Keynesians doubt whether this explanation goes to the root of the problem since other countries have resorted to 'stops' in order to deal with deficits in their balance of payments without suffering such adverse consequences. Some economists regard excessive government expenditure as the chief cause, because it has diverted resources from investment in industries producing marketable goods and services including exports. They generally go on to argue that, apart from the ever-increasing growth in the share of national expenditure taken by trades and services that serve a collective demand, official intervention in the investment decisions of firms that supply the market has directed large quantities of capital to bolstering up declining industries, or to costly prestige projects, or to ventures for which the gestation period has been excessively long. All these criticisms have been levelled against errors committed by successive governments in monetary, fiscal and industrial policy. But other economists find Britain's chief weakness to lie in incompetent industrial and commercial management, the absence of imaginative entre-preneurship, and defects in her social organisation and social attitudes which reveal themselves most obviously in her troubled industrial relations. For them the errors of government are taken to be symptoms of a deep-seated social malady.

American economists' criticism of British economy

During the 1950s and 1960s the centre of the stage, in this debate, was occupied by monetary, fiscal and exchange policies and by the problem of demand management. Sir Roy Harrod's *The British Economy*, published in 1963 and designed mainly for the enlightenment of American readers, for example, leaves the impression that Britain's troubles could be attributed almost wholly to mistakes in financial policy. He called the crisis of 1957 'bogus' and condemned the remedies applied by the then Con-servative Government as unnecessary and positively harmful. His was a fairly typical diagnosis. In the discussion of recent years financial policy, though still a target for critics, has engaged less of the economists' attention. But, as the range of the discussion has extended, the diagnosis has become less confident. This indecision is well illustrated by two widely publicised contributions to the debate. In 1968 the Brookings Institution of Washington issued the results of its comprehensive study of the British economy.[4] The main conclusion of its team of American economists was that the relatively poor performance of Britain could not be imputed primarily to faults in demand management. There were criticisms of this management in detail, but the main causes were to be found in the 'general inefficiencies pervading the economy'. Professor R. E. Caves, who led the team, put it thus :

> '. . . the potential gains in real growth from changes in demand management have been over-estimated and the extent to which the attainable growth rate has been constrained by inefficiency under-estimated.'[5]

British economists neglect the fundamentals

In 1970 a group of British economists conferred with some of the Americans who had prepared the Brookings report, and the results of their conference were published in a book edited by Sir Alec Cairncross, *Britain's Economic Prospects Reconsidered.* Here Britain's performance and prospects were reassessed in the light of recent experience, and another effort was made to explain why her growth rate had been so much lower than that of other leading industrial countries. Again, all the aspects of the subject were examined with scholarly care—demand management, investment, fiscal and monetary policy, trade and international payments, labour problems and industrial policy. What emerged from this expert scrutiny was disappointing to those who believe that economic inquiry can produce prescriptions for prosperity. Sir Alec, a former British Government economic adviser, was in the end forced to conclude not only that there was no easy cure for the 'British disease' but that its causes remained obscure and that no confident advice could be given to the government on how to set things right.

A reader of this book may be left wondering whether there is not more than a grain of truth in the gibe that a country's

---

[4] Richard E. Caves and Associates, *Britain's Economic Prospects*, Allen & Unwin, 1968.

[5] R. E. Caves, 'Second Thoughts on Britain's Economic Prospects', in Sir Alec Cairncross (ed.), *Britain's Economic Prospects Reconsidered*, Allen & Unwin, 1971, p. 212.

economic progress is in inverse proportion to the distinction of its economists! The truth is that economists tend, very naturally, when dealing with practical problems, to direct their attention to facets that can be illuminated by the methods of inquiry they find congenial. Their instruments are efficient within a range; but they often choose to ignore what lies outside it. 'What they don't know isn't knowledge', or, at any rate, not knowledge that concerns them. So it happens that, on occasions, their inquiries do not penetrate beyond the periphery of fundamental problems.[6]

An uneasy feeling that this may have been so seems to have pervaded several of the contributions to *Britain's Economic Prospects Reconsidered*. The possibility, for instance, that institutional factors and social attitudes and purposes are often decisive in economic development hovered in the background. There were references to 'intangibles', such as the practices and attitudes of managers and workers. The impact of the British social system on economic efficiency and industrial relations was also mentioned. Sir Alec, in his summary, asserted that

'the long-run relationships that should form the basis of growth policy seem to rest on social and political values at least as heavily as on economic variables.'[7]

The fundamental questions

Yet, despite the recognition of their importance, these matters received only cursory treatment. The impulsion of national purpose,

'the Opinion and Will of a People exerting them to Industry'

(to quote Berkeley's words),[8] are quickly passed by. Such neglect is inexcusable if it is indeed in these regions that the springs of progress are to be found. The questions that suggest themselves are manifold:

6 Professor M. M. Postan has been much harsher than this in his criticism of economists; he thinks that much of their influence on policy since the war has been mischievous in its effects: M. M. Postan, 'A Plague of Economists', in *Fact and Relevance: Essays on Historical Method*, Cambridge University Press, 1971, pp. 80–91. The author shares his view that the macro-economic remedies prescribed have often been inappropriate and that economists would enhance their usefulness if they paid more attention to micro-economic problems, in the solution of which they should be associated with scientists, technologists, business men and others with expert knowledge of aspects of the problems. However, Professor Postan may have under-estimated the extent of this association in post-war inquiries affecting government policy.
7 Cairncross, *op. cit.*, p. 220.
8 George Berkeley, *The Querist* (1735), Qu. 33.

—All men, except saints who court poverty, would like to be better off than they are, but are the contemporary British ready to submit to the necessary exertions and changes in their ways?

—Have not the most economically progressive countries since the Second World War consisted of those whose energies have been concentrated on growth, in contrast to Britain who has wasted her strength in pursuit of a variety of inconsistent aims?

—If it is true that Britain's social and economic institutions and attitudes are out of tune with the requirements of modern industrialism, how has this come about?

—If the quality of investment, public and private, has been low (which suggests a lack of capacity among the decision-makers), does this point to defects in the selection and training of civil servants and business executives?

—Finally, and not least, why has the British system of industrial relations become so anachronistic as to excite derision among people who once looked to Britain as their model?

The present author believes that it is in these regions that economists must look for most of the causes of Britain's economic plight. Moreover, it is not sufficient to confine attention to the contemporary scene. One must trace the deficiencies to their source in order to understand how she lost her way.

II. GOVERNMENT POLICY, BUREAUCRACY AND INDUSTRY

Let us begin this inquiry by considering the capitalisation of industry and the relevance of institutional arrangements and attitudes to the quantity and quality of investment. It is a common assertion in economic discussion, especially among trade union leaders and politicians, that international differences in the rate of growth are closely correlated with differences in investment. Output per head of British workers, it is claimed, is lower than among workers of the United States, Western Germany and Japan because of the disparities in the capital equipment available to the workforce in the several countries. The gap has been widening in recent years through the relatively low rate of Britain's investment, especially in manufacturing industry. The remedy according to the more simplistic politicians, is to pump more money, supplied largely by the Exchequer, into the purchase of new plant.

Inadequacy of investment? A (qualified) red herring

This diagnosis can be accepted only with qualifications, and the remedy not at all. In the first place, very important advances in productivity have been achieved without the investment of additional capital and simply by the more effective use of the capital already installed. Let us take a few historical examples. The rise in the output per man-shift in the German coal industry during the 1930s, a rise which put the Germans far ahead of the British in coal productivity, was not attributable to the installation of more, or more elaborate, mining equipment, for most of the German mines had been fully mechanised before 1930. The chief cause was the improved organisation of mining operations, in other words, more intelligent management.[9]

The rise in average productivity in the British coal-mining industry during the last 25 years has not been held back by a shortage of capital; investment in mining has, on the contrary, been very substantial. What has prevented productivity from rising more rapidly has been the policy followed for many years of maintaining production in the high-cost mines in South Wales, Scotland and elsewhere, when the efficient operation of the industry required the concentration of production on the rich mining areas of the East Midlands. Cross-subsidisation in keeping going the high-cost mines at the expense of the efficient meant that capital was wasted and that coal was more expensive and wages lower than they would have been if a rational and more ruthless policy had been followed. It was not followed for social and political reasons.

Management efficiency and worker attitudes

Again, the Building Industry Working Party that reported in 1950 pointed out that the higher productivity of the American workers compared with the British did not depend mainly on the superior equipment available to the former. The advantage came, first, from the way the Americans organised the whole complex of building operations from the time the contract was

---

[9] *Report of the Technical Advisory Committee on Coal Mining* (1945), pp. 24, 37.

let until the completion of the building and, secondly, from the attitude of the operatives to their work.[10] The Elstub Committee on the Aircraft Industry (1967–9) noted that, although the *wages* of the American aircraft workers were about three times those of the British, their productivity was also three times larger, so that American *wage-costs* were not higher. It is true that this superiority was determined largely by such factors as the size of the orders for particular aircraft which enabled expenditure on research and development to be spread over a larger output and also reduced the incidence of the 'learning period'. But the quality of management, especially middle management, and the attitudes of the workers towards their work, contributed heavily to the high American performance.[11] Furthermore, the achievement by a producer of a long run on an aircraft must not be regarded as independent of the efficiency with which an enterprise is conducted; indeed, it is, in part, a function of marketing and administrative skill.

Nor does success in the manufacture of aircraft depend solely on the producing firms. Public administration is also involved, for decisions about what is to be produced rest, of course, with a number of government departments and the nationalised air services. The ineptitude shown in this connection by the authorities is widely recognised. The muddle over the first version of the Trident and the deplorable history of the TSR2 are only two examples. The huge waste of resources that resulted from the decision to build Concorde call in question the government's judgement in reaching decisions in matters of high technology. Concorde certainly lends force to Mr Michael Posner's contention that there has been 'an excessive British tendency to back technological horses before they are really fit to run'.[12] Another example of the government's technological inadequacy is provided by the history of atomic energy. The lead that Britain gained in the development of atomic energy for civil use (largely through the genius and devotion of a small group of scientists and engineers in the public service) was thrown away by subsequent

10 *Report of Working Party on Building Industry, passim*; also Marian Bowley, The *British Building Industry*, Cambridge University Press, 1966, p. 441.
11 *Report of Committee on Productivity of National Aircraft Effort* (Sir John Elstub), HMSO, 1969: 'The ratio of fixed capital to turnover is not so very different in the two countries [UK and USA]. A high ratio of fixed capital to labour employed could be produced simply by greater efficiency in the use of labour as a result of better labour practices, shop floor management and production control' (para. 289).
12 Cairncross, *op. cit.*, p. 160.

maladministration; the government handed over to consortia of firms productive responsibilities which proved to be beyond their capacity. The waste of capital by the mishandling of projects of a technologically advanced type[13] was matched by the large sums of public money poured into decaying industries and loss-making firms : for example, Upper Clyde Shipbuilders, motor-cycle production, machine-tool firms, British Leyland, and several others. The loss of capital incurred in coercing firms to set up new production in unsuitable areas for social or political reasons will be discussed later (p. 29).

The conclusion is, first, that more investment is not the only road to higher productivity and, secondly, that additional investment if unwisely directed will detract from, rather than improve, the country's economic performance. In the end the question remains : Why has investment been so seriously mismanaged since the war?

Politicians and civil servants

No doubt much of the blame must lie with the politicians. But the civil servants, whose voice is, to say the least, very influential, cannot escape responsibility, for they have not distinguished themselves in handling the technological and economic problems presented to them. The questions must be posed, therefore, whether their selection and training may not have been at fault, or whether the process by which decisions are made in the government or public sector has been defective. Before these questions are examined, however, there is more to be said about the causes of disparity among the nations in investment.

So far, the argument has been concerned with the quality of investment, and it has left quite undisturbed the proposition that a high rate of wisely directed investment is a major factor in growth. This is not equivalent to saying that investment is the source and origin of prosperity, for high investment is as much the *result* as the *cause* of growth. It is in a country where production and incomes are rising fast that the stimulus to investment is strongest and the resources needed are most readily available. The conspicuously rapid growth of Japan and West Germany during the 1950s cannot be ascribed to their possession of large liquid resources available for investment, for at the

[13] John Jewkes, *Government and High Technology*, Third Wincott Memorial Lecture, published as Occasional Paper 37, IEA, 1972.

beginning of that decade their economies were still struggling to emerge from the ruins of war, and capital was very scarce. Yet, by concentrating their energies on growth to the virtual exclusion at first of other ends, they set going an economic revival which gathered momentum as time went on. Once their GNP began to rise, a 'virtuous circle' came into being; increasing production brought higher real incomes which provided the means for increased saving and investment and so led to still higher production. Such a policy required the investment of a very high proportion of their national income (35 per cent in Japan during the 1960s). Yet the investment could not be said to have been at the expense of consumption, except in the very short run, for the increased production that attended the policy was soon accompanied by a steep increase in personal incomes.

The experience of these countries has another lesson to teach. The success of their policy in creating the 'virtuous circle' depended upon their directing a large share of their investment into forms of capital that yielded their returns *quickly* in marketable goods and service. The rise in money incomes was thus accompanied by an increase in the quantity of goods and services available for consumption. In Britain the investment took a different form. Much of it was embodied in capital which yielded low returns or returns in the distant future. It has been argued that an excessive amount of public investment has been directed into administrative services or into projects that supply a collective demand and are exempt from the competitive test of efficiency.[14] In other words, if economic growth was the objective, many of the investments were ill-chosen.[15]

The quality of economic decision-makers is crucial, especially for innovation

The key to development, so this argument suggests, is in the hands of those who take the main decisions on policy. That is to say, the quality of economic leadership is crucial. In countries like the USA, Germany and Japan, where entrepreneurs find the environment congenial to the display of their talents, obstacles

---

[14] Cf. R. W. Bacon and W. A. Eltis, 'Stop-Go and De-Industrialisation', and D. Smith, 'Public Consumption and Economic Performance', in *National Westminster Bank Quarterly Review*, November 1975.

[15] Some considerable investment in the infra-structure is, of course, essential in a modern industrial society, if merely to serve the needs of the market-orientated industries. Japan for a long time neglected the former and has lately been obliged to restore a balance. It is a question of degree.

to progress are quickly overcome. In the presence of high enterprise the capital needed is seldom lacking.

The function of the entrepreneur, whether an individual or a team, is not simply the efficient management of established productive and marketing processes. His capacity is to be judged, like that of the economy as a whole, by success in innovation. Schumpeter drew a famous distinction between the 'routineer' among business men and the true entrepreneur who demonstrates his exceptional quality by his skill in effecting new combinations of resources, often for the production of new classes of goods or services.[16] Before Schumpeter, Alfred Marshall had pointed to the contrast between those business men who

'have prospered by steady adherence to affairs, largely of a routine character, with but little use of the higher imagination . . .'

and the leaders

'on whose work the progress of industry most depends'.[17]

P. W. S. Andrews, in his book on business behaviour, emphasised the special importance of the part played in industrial progress by the 'surging energy of the founder-type of personality'.[18] The function of the true entrepreneur may reside in an individual, or a group of individuals, including the salaried officers of a company. It is a function that may, on occasion, be discharged by a civil servant of exceptional quality. The presence of such men in positions of authority will confer on the economy a readiness to change course, to re-allocate resources as technology and markets alter.

That structural adaptability is a condition of economic progress has been demonstrated convincingly by the history of development, and the proposition received powerful support from the research of W. E. G. Salter. It showed that, between 1924 and 1950, increases in average productivity could be ascribed mainly to a small number of very progressive industries. The conclusion was inescapable for a country really intent upon economic and social improvement:

'Policies to raise productivity should . . . ensure a climate where

[16] This is a theme of Schumpeter's *The Theory of Economic Development*, Harvard University Press, 1934 (OUP reprint, 1961).
[17] A. C. Pigou (ed.), *Memorials of Alfred Marshall*, Macmillan, 1925, p. 331.
[18] P. W. S. Andrews, *Manufacturing Business*, Macmillan, 1949, p. 284.

expanding industries are not hampered in their growth and
declining industries are not artificially supported.'[19]

In the genesis and expansion of the progressive industries
industrial leaders of high quality have been the driving force.
Their influence, if they are allowed scope, permeates the economy
as a whole. They set the pace, drawing after them the 'routineers',
whose old markets are destroyed, or whose methods are rendered
obsolete, by the innovations. Those who cannot follow fall out
of the race.

British economic policies have obstructed adaptation to change

I have suggested that British industrial policy has for a long time
been hostile to change; that, through the influence of the government, capital has been dissipated in bolstering up inefficient,
established industries, and that human resources have been
wasted by measures designed to maintain employment in declining manufactures and so to retard their transference to more
productive uses. It may be objected that, despite official and trade
union efforts to resist change, a re-distribution of labour on a
large scale has taken place in Britain since the Second World
War as well as in more progressive countries. To this objection
there is a two-fold reply.

First, re-allocation in itself has no merit unless it means
the transference of resources from low-productivity to high-
productivity occupations. Here Britain can be seriously faulted,
for during the last decade an increasing proportion of labour
had found its way into occupations that serve some administrative need but add little or nothing to the production of marketable
goods and services. Secondly, the re-deployment *among industries*
that was necessary to achieve an efficient distribution of resources
was far more extensive in Britain than among her rivals, chiefly
because she lacked the large reserves of rural labour available to
the majority of them. Of all countries she could least afford to
apply a brake on the progressive in the interests of maintaining
the *status quo*, and her defence of the old-fashioned and obsolete
slowed down her transition to a modern, high-technology
economy. How Britain became a captive to this restrictionist,
conservative policy will be examined presently (pp. 51–54). At
this point it is necessary to consider the official attitude to
industrial leadership in a wider context.

[19] W. E. G. Salter, *Productivity and Technical Change*, Cambridge University Press, 1961, p. 155.

Government and public attitudes to leadership in industry

Government policy reflects, often with distortions, the will of the people, and there can be little doubt that, for a variety of reasons, public opinion has become increasingly suspicious of the exercise of industrial leadership. Here may be one of the germs of the British malady. Eighty years ago Alfred Marshall noted that, while economic progress did not necessarily require the maintenance of those rights of property that lead to extreme inequalities of wealth, it did depend on the existence of a social milieu sympathetic to the exercise of free, individual responsibility.[20] Later, in his *Industry and Trade* (1921), he suggested that, in those days, the United States satisfied that condition more completely than this country.

'As arts and sciences flourish best where their followers work for the approval of the brethren of the craft . . ., so business flourishes most where the aim of the business man is . . . to be held in respect of those who are the best judges of his special form of strength.'[21]

About the same time Sir William Ashley said that the social prestige enjoyed by American business leaders was one of the reasons why a high proportion of the most able young Americans from the Universities sought careers in industry and commerce.[22] During the last 20 years Japan has provided the best example of countries where business men are held in high regard. They have enjoyed public acclaim as the agents of the policy of rapid growth which has been remarkably successful in raising the standard of living of the whole nation. To the ordinary Japanese they are as well known as pop stars to the ordinary young Englishman. The newspapers organise public-opinion polls in which the qualities and appeal of the several leaders are rated. It is significant that those who occupy the top places are the entrepreneurs who have founded great new industries, especially those like Mr K. Matsushita and Mr S. Honda who have risen from modest beginnings by their own genius and energy.

'This popularity', declare the authors of a recent book on Japanese business, 'indicates the strength of one of the factors

20 A. C. Pigou (ed.), *op. cit.*, p. 282. This was a theme of Marshall's Presidential Address to the Economics, Science and Statistics section of the British Association in 1890.
21 Alfred Marshall, *Industry and Trade*, Macmillan, 1921, p. 156.
22 W. J. Ashley, *Commercial Education*, Williams and Norgate, 1926, pp. 97 *et seq.*

which helps to stimulate entrepreneurs to become national heroes and to know that they work for the national good.'[23]

The attitude of contemporary Japanese to their business leaders may recall that of early Victorian admirers of Samuel Smiles's industrial biographies.

There is more than a hint in the story of Japan's industrial success of motives that are rooted elsewhere than in personal self-interest, compelling though that may have been. One certainly cannot understand her achievements without reference to patriotic motives. Mr S. Honda's own words furnish an illustration. When just after the Second World War he was beginning to build up his company, he was criticised for what appeared to be his recklessness in pushing ahead with expansion. To this charge he replied:

'Even if my business were to go bankrupt because I expand my plant too fast, the plant itself will remain to be of use for the development of Japanese industry.'

Such an attitude would not have surprised Alfred Marshall who wrote: 'Some touch of idealism, religious, patriotic or artistic, can generally be detected at the root of any great outburst of practical energy.'[24] Of course, 'patriotism is not enough' for success; it must be served by shrewdness and calculation. Honda's struggles and ultimate achievement as a pioneer recalls another of Marshall's penetrating comments on the distinctive contribution of the private entrepreneur to economic progress. Any alternative to private enterprise, he warned, must provide some

'reasonably efficient substitute for the freedom which that system offered to constructive genius to work its way to the light and to prove its existence by attempting difficult tasks on its own responsibility and succeeding in them; for those who have done most for the world have seldom been those whom their neighbours would have picked out as likely for the work.'[25]

Bureaucratic involvement has worsened relations between industry and government

The creation of an environment favourable to industrial enter-

---

[23] J. Hirschmeier and T. Yui, *The Development of Japanese Business*, Allen and Unwin, 1975, p. 254.
[24] Alfred Marshall, *op. cit.*, p. 161.
[25] A. C. Pigou (ed.), *op. cit.*, p. 284.

prise may well have been the government's chief contribution to economic success in countries which have prospered since the war, notably in West Germany and lately in France where policy has been worked out in co-operation with industry, having economic expansion as a prime objective. In Britain the relations between industry and government have deteriorated progressively as the bureaucratic involvement in the economy has intensified. This is attributable largely to the nature and purpose of official intervention. Far from being directed towards the stimulation of innovation and commercial success, it has generally been guided by motives that are indifferent to economic efficiency. Some great industries after 1945 became a pawn in the political game.

Consider the steel industry which was partly nationalised in 1950, de-nationalised in 1953, and finally re-nationalised in 1966. Even in its so-called free-enterprise stage it was subject to official control in pricing, investment and the location of its plants, and one result of this control was to hamper its adjustment to market and technical changes. Again the motor industry, in the interests of regional policy rather than of manufacturing efficiency, was coerced into establishing new capacity in high-cost locations. According to a leading motor manufacturer,[26] the decision that obliged him to locate one of his new plants in Scotland meant an increase of costs equivalent to the profit he would have expected to earn on the production of a particular model on the site he preferred.

A location-of-industry policy is no doubt a necessary part of a country's economic strategy, but if those who administer it brush aside the objections of industrialists to particular decisions and justify their action by reference to the pretentious uncertainties of cost-benefit analysis, the competitive strength of the industry is likely to be damaged. The present plight of the steel and motor industries has been brought about by a complex of causes, but government's rash decisions on location are certainly among them. The official industrial policy has also affected fashion in organisation. At a time when large size was held to be a condition of competitive efficiency, the government's influence was used to bring about several combinations. The subsequent career of the most important of these (British Leyland) suggests that the intervention was misguided in at least one instance.

[26] Cf. Lord Stokes, then Chairman and Managing Director of British Leyland, in evidence to the Trade and Industry Sub-Committee of the House of Commons Expenditure Committee, HC No. 347, July 1972.

In conflicts with the bureaucracy the British industrialist has not been able to count on popular support for, in the post-war world, he has ranked low in popular esteem. His 'special form of strength', to quote Marshall's phrase, does not now command social approbation. The contrast between Britain and Japan in this respect could hardly be sharper. The consequence is that, at a time when the British manager is probably better trained and more professionally expert than ever before, he finds himself struggling in a society generally unsympathetic to his function. If he is successful he is denounced as an exploiter; if his business is a loss-maker he is derided as an incompetent. So his morale has suffered. Many influences have combined to produce this public attitude and a comprehensive examination of them lies beyond the horizon of this *Paper*. But it may be suggested that an important contributory cause has been that in Britain the teachers, journalists, broadcast producers and others who have done most to form opinion have been brought up and educated in circles with few contacts with the country's industrial life.

III. GENESIS OF DECLINE IN 19TH CENTURY

The argument so far has suggested that the deterioration in Britain's economic position in recent years can be attributed in some considerable part to mistakes in government policy. But the country was in trouble long before state intervention in industrial affairs was of significance or the public sector absorbed much of the national income.[27]

Early weakening of Britain's industrial lead

As early as the 1870s there were signs that Britain's industrial supremacy was being challenged and by the end of the century she had lost the lead in several branches of production. Some economists were disquieted about her future for reasons that had little to do with her competence in manufacturing. Jevons, even in the 1860s, was troubled by the increasing cost of mining the coal on which the country's prosperity had rested.[28] Early in the

---

[27] In the first decade of the century it was probably only about 10 per cent.
[28] W. S. Jevons, *The Coal Question*, Macmillan, Second Edition, 1866, pp. v–vii.

new century, Marshall thought that her 'age of economic grace'[29] might be drawing to its close because of a worsening in Britain's terms of trade. But others traced the cause of her failure to keep pace with foreign rivals to antiquated methods of production and marketing and a lack of expertise among her business leaders. Sir William Ashley, in *The Tariff Problem* (1902), warned his generation that 'all the older staple industries of Great Britain are either visibly declining or maintaining themselves with increasing difficulty'. He referred to the development of manufactures in countries previously supplied by Britain and he observed that, in many cases, these manufactures were being conducted more efficiently than here. It seemed to him that Britain's relative advantages as an international trader were increasingly to be found only in coal, an irreplaceable raw material, or in trades that depended on her resources of cheap labour. The rest was threatened by German applied science and American mass-production.[30]

Ashley was not alone in his alarm. The Tariff Commission of 1904 reported on the failure of the British iron and steel producers to operate on a scale that might have enabled them to remain competitive with the Americans.[31] Some blast furnaces in the United States produced 200,000–220,000 tons of pig iron a year, whereas the average annual output of British furnaces was only 28,000 tons. The British seemed to be slow in introducing automatic machinery and, partly in consequence, productivity throughout most branches of American industry had risen far above that of British industry. In shipbuilding Britain still held the lead, but it rested in the new century on the import of cheap Continental steel. The progress of the cotton industry, though slower than in its heyday, continued because it had been possible to find what proved to be ephemeral new markets in the East to compensate for the loss of exports to Western countries. But of all the older industries Britain's deficiencies had become most apparent in chemicals. She had been a pioneer in this manufacture and her chemists had been responsible for some of the most important recent discoveries. Yet as a manufacturer she had been overtaken by Germany and Switzerland by the early years

---

29 A. C. Pigou (ed.), *op. cit.*, p. 326.
30 W. J. Ashley, *The Tariff Problem*, P. S. King, 1902, p. 112.
31 Report of the Tariff Commission (1904): Vol. 1, *The Iron and Steel Trades.*

of the 20th century and her textile manufactures had become almost entirely dependent on German dyes.[32]

Failure to take the lead in new industries

It was probably inevitable that Britain should lose her predominant position in all the older manufactures as other countries industrialised, and it was by her failure to secure a large share of the newer trades then coming into being rather than by her loosening her hold on some of the old industries that Britain's weaknesses were becoming most obvious in the years before the First World War. Two industries were to become of outstanding importance. In motor cars Britain by 1914 ranked as a poor second to the United States. In electrical equipment she was surpassed by both the United States and Germany. The same applied to the manufacture of automatic machine-tools. A government committee that reported in 1918 made similar criticisms. In the years immediately before the war the UK had taken a very limited share in the rise and expansion of the more modern branches of industrial production,

'as is evidenced by our relative weakness in respect of the electrical, chemical and chemico-metallurgical industries; and it is admitted that in a number of smaller trades foreign manufacturers had shown greater enterprise and originality'.[33]

It is significant that many of the entrepreneurs in the newer lines of production at that time did not come from the well-established firms in those industries which might have seemed their most likely parents. Thus, at the beginning of the motor age, the larger engineering firms were sceptical of the prospects of the motor vehicle and left the development of the industry to pioneers from electrical engineering, cycle making and repairing, tinplate-ware manufacture and sheep-shearing machinery production. Many of these firms were very small at the outset. Similarly, rayon manufacture was introduced not by any of the major firms in the great textile industries but by a specialist silk weaver who happened at a critical moment to have in his employment an imaginative chemist.

How can we explain this slackening in Britain's industrial

---

[32] The outbreak of war in 1914 led to an immediate shortage of several other products essential for the conduct of the war, such as acetone for explosives and magnetos for transport, since Germany had become their chief source of supply.

[33] *Final Report of Committee on Commercial and Industrial Policy after the War*, Cd. 9035, 1918, XIII, paras. 93–4, 96–9.

growth in this period? The once ample supply of cheap rural labour available for manning industry was drying up but labour, skilled as well as other kinds, was certainly not scarce. Some critics have put the blame on Britain's financial organisation : the pre-occupation of the London capital market with overseas investments (so it is claimed) deprived domestic industry of the capital it needed for modernisation.[34] Yet in those days manufacturing firms seldom made public issues. They usually built up their resources from the re-investment of profits and in the industrial areas there were many other channels through which enterprising manufacturers could obtain capital. Even the British banks, often contrasted unfavourably with the German banks as sources of investment funds for industry, were by no means so aloof as is often made out. In the early 1900s the managing director of Midland Bank, having taken the measure of a hitherto unknown supplicant, had little hesitation in advancing a huge sum to put GEC on the road to success. If the London capital market was often less forthcoming, this attitude cannot be ascribed wholly to institutional defects; it may be explained by the generally unimpressive quality of Britain's industrial leaders at that time. The reluctance was probably wholly justified, for the rise in the amount of capital per head invested in industry after 1900 was not accompanied by any increase in productivity.[35]

It was unfortunate that at a time when entrepreneurial initiative in British industry was flagging, the law became more favourable than hitherto towards conspiracies of traders to promote their commercial interests and towards contracts in restraint of trade. This change, which occurred as a result of a series of Court decisions, confirmed by the famous Mogul judgement of 1892, provided firms with additional safeguards against competitive pressure and opened the way to restrictive practices of various kinds. However, as long as the country remained faithful to free trade, the power of such cartels and monopolies as were formed was necessarily weak in the large number of industries exposed to foreign competition in the home market. Indeed, in Germany cartelisation was carried much further than in Britain, and in the British industries that depended mainly on foreign

---

[34] A. R. Hall, 'A Note on the English capital market as a source of funds for home investment before 1914', *Economica*, February 1957; also W. H. B. Court, *British Economic History, 1870–1914*, Cambridge University Press, 1965, p. 80 and *passim*.

[35] W. H. B. Court, *ibid.*, Chap. 3, for a penetrating discussion of economic development in this period.

markets a strongly competitive character was preserved. How was it, then, that the competition failed to keep the member-firms in these industries up to the mark? The answer may be that, while free competition is highly effective in transforming potential entrepreneurial energy into kinetic energy, its capacity to *create* the potential is limited. This at any rate seems a reasonable inference from the industrial experience of the period.

The unconventional wisdom of Schumpeter may throw light on this problem. In a well-known passage, he declared that the kind of competition that counts is

> 'the competition from the new commodity, the new technology, the new source of supply, the new type of organisation—competition which commands a decisive cost or quality advantage and which strikes not simply at the margin of the profits and output of existing firms, but at their foundations and their very lives'.[36]

What he called 'the gale of creative destruction', which, according to him, was the really powerful agent of change and progress in a dynamic society, not least in Britain between, say, 1760 and 1870, seems to have blown itself out in the industry of this country by the last years of the 19th century.

We are thus led back to the proposition that industrial progress depends primarily on the quality of industrial leadership and we have to consider whether that quality had deteriorated since the great days and, if so, for what reasons. Evidence must be sought in many directions, especially in managerial recruitment and training, social attitudes and education.

Complacency by descendants of pioneers

Complacency after a long period of success was perhaps to be expected. As Arnold Toynbee said : 'History shows that the group which successfully responds to one challenge is rarely the successful respondent to the next.'[37] The descendants of the pioneers are tempted to take things easy. The institutions created to serve one stage of development may prove to be intractable and frustrating at the next stage, but may survive nonetheless through the force of tradition and convention.[38] This generalisation seems

---

[36] J. A. Schumpeter, *Capitalism, Socialism and Democracy*, Allen & Unwin: Unwin University Books (12th Impression 1970), p. 84.
[37] *A Study of History*, Royal Institute of International Affairs, Abridged Edition, 1960, p. 927.
[38] *Ibid.*, pp. 925–6.

to describe what happened in Britain, and the development did not pass unremarked by critical contemporaries, especially those aware of what was happening in other countries. Kipling's bitter rebuke to his fellow-countrymen in the poem, *The Islanders* (1902), was intended to stir them from their complacency in defence; it would have been equally well justified if directed against their economic and technical deficiencies. Yet the gadflies failed to pierce the thick hide of the Edwardians. B. Bowker, in his *Lancashire Under the Hammer*, gave a superb example of the unshatterable self-esteem of business men during the Indian summer of the British export trade. He recalled an occasion in 1911 when he was referring to the loss of Lancashire's market in Japan through the competition of domestic producers. A cotton manufacturer who heard his remarks rounded on him in indignation :

> 'My lad, never again let anybody in Lancashire hear you talk this childish stuff about foreign competition. It's right enough for Londoners and such like, but it puts a born Lancashire man to shame as an ignoramus. It's just twaddle. In the first place, we've got the only climate in the world where cotton piece goods in any quantity can ever be produced. In the second, no foreign Johnnies can ever be bred that can spin and weave like Lancashire lads and lasses. In the third place, there are more spindles in Oldham than in all the rest of the world put together. And last of all, if they had the climate and the men and the spindles—which they never can have—foreigners could never find the brains Lancashire cotton men have for the job.'[39]

In 1922 I received precisely the same assurance of Lancashire's enduring superiority from a young representative of a Manchester firm I met in Singapore on my way to Japan : Britain would soon regain the markets she had temporarily lost through the interruption of supplies during the war ! A year later, in Japan itself, I was assured by a group of British aeronautical engineers, engaged by the Japanese to build aircraft, that Orientals had no 'feeling' for machinery and were ham-handed as pilots. They would never excel as engineers.

Disdain for trade

Besides the general causes of decadence which, according to

[39] B. Bowker, *Lancashire Under the Hammer*, L. and V. Woolf, 1928, pp. 22-3.

Toynbee, are likely to afflict every civilisation in some stage of its development, there were present in Britain some special, and perhaps rather extraordinary, causes that converged to transform so many of the heirs of the great industrial innovators into complacent routineers. In order to analyse these we must make a brief excursion into English social history. In England, unlike some Western societies before the French Revolution and many Asian societies, rigid divisions between castes, each with its appropriate functions, did not exist. The Tudors and those that came after them held that a man must do 'his duty in that state of life into which it *shall* please God to call him', and a man of ambition found his fulfilment in ensuring that he was called to a higher class than that into which he was born. In the 17th century, after the country was launched on its career as an international trader, those who made money as merchants naturally sought to elevate themselves into the class above them, the landed gentry. This was the path to social esteem and political and administrative power. They purchased country estates and married their daughters to the sons of the squires. Once the merchant families were established in their new class, they did their best to forget their origins. An historian has pointed out that, whereas the Elizabethan and Jacobean monuments in the parish churches record the origin of many a squire's wealth in his prosperity as a mercer or haberdasher, from Queen Anne's time there were few parallels.

> 'The more commercial England in fact became, the more general was the contempt for trade among the landed gentry who were themselves largely its offspring; ... it was among the children of these rich, retired tradesmen that there sprang up such a contempt for whatever savoured of the shop or the counting house.'[40]

Anti-manufacturing snobbery

The tradition of snobbism was transmitted intact to the new wealthy families of industrialists who rose on the tide of Britain's manufacturing supremacy in the 19th century. They too delighted 'to play the sedulous ape' to the landed gentry. Their ambition to adopt the habits and manners of their betters provided a

[40] W. J. Ashley, *The Economic Organisation of England* (1914), pp. 130–1. The distaste for business among those who had recently acquired gentility did not always extend to the aristocracy, for in the 18th century as in earlier times some landed magnates (such as the Dudleys) were active in promoting enterprises in the coal and iron industries.

splendid opportunity for alert educationists. Hence the proliferation of the public boarding schools after the time of Thomas Arnold. The schools proved to be an effective instrument for bestowing gentility on the sons of the rough and warty industrial pioneers, and their vitality down to the present time can be attributed to the persistence of the same type of social ambition. Continental Europeans have seized on what is only a half-truth when they explain the existence of these boarding schools by their theory that the English dislike their children. André Maurois showed a more accurate perception in his comment that the schools were a means for inculcating the prejudices of a class.

Strengths and faults of public schools vis-à-vis industry

The public schools would not, of course, have flourished if they had not also served loftier purposes. They had great merits as the nursery of political leaders and administrators for several generations, and their products proved their mettle in the government of the British Empire. The standards of behaviour they inculcated were a marked improvement on those of the aristocracy in earlier times. The men they trained helped to bring order and a large measure of fair dealing over much of the globe, and the infra-structure which they built up in the under-developed countries was a major legacy of Britain to the successor states of her Empire. In a word, the schools helped to form an élite, with the character and self-confidence appropriate to the needs of Britain as an Imperial Power. The members of this élite were taught to accept a special responsibility for serving the common weal, and this responsibility the best of them bore without arrogance. Perhaps because of their isolation from their fellows in other classes during their formative years, they may have found it all too easy to reconcile their personal ambitions, their desire for power and the maintenance of their privileged status, with their idea of themselves as Platonic Guardians, but they were not alone in confusing personal advantage and the common good. The chief weakness of the schools, when judged from the standpoint of the present inquiry, was their failure to provide leaders equipped to manage Britain's economy in general, and her industry in particular, in an era when her former commercial supremacy was waning. Their deficiencies in this respect became more evident with the passing of empire, but they had been perceived long ago by critics troubled by the early signs of Britain's economic decline. The schools even instilled a distaste for the pursuits which had made the country rich and powerful. Their most able pupils made their careers in politics, the Civil Service and the professions. Too few of them entered business life.[41]

Professor M. M. Postan's brilliant survey of the industrial manager in Europe leads him to conclusions that parallel those suggested here. Despite the appearance of a few energetic entrepreneurs in the newer industries, industrial leaders of the type classified

> 'as "parochial" or "traditional" had established themselves as the predominant type in most of the older British industries . . . In cotton, wool, linen, coal, steel, shipbuilding and a host of other old-established trades it was possible to conduct business and make profits without venturing into new attitudes and methods.'[42]

Bowker, writing of the cotton industry before the First World War, put the point more harshly : 'At this time a man who couldn't make cotton pay had to be in some way mentally deficient.'[43] Many firms in the staple industries were being run by men in the second, third and fourth generation of the founders' families. A large number of these men had acquired, through a conventional public school education,

> 'the tastes and attitudes of the leisured classes and were prepared to leave the day-to-day conduct of the firms to shop-floor managers who were frequently promoted foremen, themselves workmen brought up in the existing methods of production and wedded to them.'[44]

Charlotte Erickson's scholarly study of the social origins and careers of British business leaders offers further supporting evidence.[45] She has shown that many of the pioneers in the 19th-

[41] In Scotland the social order and the educational system differed from those of England in several respects. That may be a reason why, once the Scots had responded to the appeal of their 'noblest prospect', they were so successful in all activities that called for energy, common-sense and trained intelligence. After all, they had only the English to compete with ! But once a typical Scot, like equally ambitious and talented immigrants from the Continent, had completed his inevitable progression to the 'commanding heights', he submitted gratefully to the embrace of England's social and educational conventions.

[42] M. M. Postan, *An Economic History of Western Europe, 1945–1964*, Methuen, 1967, p. 281. Professor Postan is here referring to Britain before 1914.

[43] B. Bowker, *op. cit.*, p. 17.

[44] M. M. Postan, *op. cit.*, pp. 283–4.

[45] C. Erickson, *British Industrialists: Steel and Hosiery, 1850–1950*, Cambridge University Press, 1959, especially Chap. II.

century steel industry, having achieved success, fell victim to the social infection which has been the source of lively contributions to the English comedy of manners, but has done much to debilitate economic leadership in this country. The prosperous steel masters, most of whom had themselves been educated in local schools, followed the now customary practice among the successful members of the business community and despatched their sons to the public schools. In many instances their families' social status was subsequently elevated by the marriage of these sons into the landed and professional classes whose outlook they acquired. High achievement in industry and commerce thus often came to be regarded as a route to the satisfaction of social aspirations. Britain, to her loss, was ceasing to produce, in the older industries at any rate, a class of leader who found sufficient scope for his ambition and adequate satisfaction for his pride, in his business accomplishments. The form of snobbery prevalent among business men may have had especially mischievous effects in steel manufacture because that industry furnished very few instances of ambitious and capable young men of humble origin whose path to managerial eminence was smoothed by the traditional and admirable expedient of marrying the boss's daughter! Of course, there were many substantial family businesses that maintained their entrepreneurial vigour from generation to generation. Examples can be found in the glass, confectionery and brewing industries among others, and these manufactures continued to make progress.

Failure of the universities to supply industrial leaders

The inadequacy of school education in equipping the new generation of industrial leaders was not remedied by the universities. Despite the founding of the civic universities at the turn of the century, the higher education of the upper-middle class was dominated by Oxford and Cambridge, and has remained so, to a diminishing extent, until the present time. The older universities had little interest in, or understanding of, industrial affairs.[46]

[46] University College London, which established a separate Faculty of Science in 1870, attracted from the older universities mature students for whom no adequate provision was made for science teaching at Oxford and Cambridge. (H. Hale Bellot, *University College London, 1826–1926* (1929), pp. 307–8.) It is significant that the founder of the now famous Massachusetts Institute of Technology (1865) drew his inspiration from the Manchester Literary and Philosophical Society and the Warrington Academy and *not* from the great English universities. (D. S. L. Cardwell, *The Organisation of Science in England*, Heinemann, Revised Edition, 1972, p. 101.)

Indeed, the educational principles, to which in the half-century before the First World War they were wedded, were not compatible with the type of training devised in other countries for men who were to occupy key positions in industry or commerce. The purpose of a university, it was held, was to make a 'whole man' and not to equip him to follow a specific calling, to prepare pupils for 'everything in general and nothing in particular'. This doctrine, in its more extreme form, declared that the more practically useless a subject, the higher its claims as an instrument for mental discipline. Mr Harold Macmillan, in his charming and moving reminiscences of Oxford in the years before the war, quotes with evident approval the opening words of a lecturer to his class. After referring to the careers they were likely to follow, the Church, the Bar, politics, the Civil Service and Army, teaching and even industry and commerce, he declared that, except for those who were to teach,

> 'nothing that you will learn in the course of your studies will be of the slightest use to you in after life, except this ... that you should be able to detect when a man is talking rot, and that in my view is the aim, if not the sole purpose, of education'.[47]

It does not seem to have occurred to Mr Macmillan that the history of Britain during the last 60 years shows that this education, in practice, provided a most ineffectual defence against the seductions of humbug and rhetoric, for one of the outstanding defects of Britain's leaders in that period has been their lack of realism in confronting the problems that faced her. He has also not perceived that the definition of education presented to him was idiosyncratic and parochial. Traditionally universities have been the home of *professional* education. In the Middle Ages they prepared men for the ecclesiastical profession and, after the rise of the nation-states, they became the home of Cameralistic studies designed to equip men to serve *religioni et reipublicae*, to quote the motto of one of the Tudor foundations. The anti-vocational bias, the concept of a general mental culture divorced from professional needs as the sole, or the chief, *raison d'être* of a university, gained wide acceptance only after Oxford and Cambridge, about a century ago, acquired a body of resident lay tutors. That this peculiar definition of the purpose of a

[47] Harold Macmillan, 'Oxford Remembered', in *The Times*, 18 October, 1975.

university survived the introduction of numerous vocational studies, as the training for the professions passed to the universities, can be ascribed mainly to the prestige of Oxford and Cambridge. The proposition that vocational training is not inconsistent with the education of the 'whole man' was considered in those quarters as unworthy of debate. In consequence, until a generation or so ago, few of those recruited into the ranks of industrial managers from the universities had received a training in subjects in any way related to their calling. In the second place, men who had been educated in vocational or professional subjects generally occupied, and still occupy, both in the Civil Service and in many of the big corporations, subordinate or advisory posts; they were seldom elevated to the ranks of the policy-makers.[48]

Vocational training in Continental universities

On the Continent and in the United States, vocational training was held to be a proper function of a university. Nor was it considered inconsistent with the education of a cultivated citizen. A leader in business or administration was not thought to be inferior for having studied subjects relevant to the work he had to do. Indeed, it was reasonable to suppose that he might be more keenly aware of modern trends and problems than a man who, in his impressionable youth, had been confined to an ivory tower.

The comparative performance of the various countries in industry and trade does not suggest that the English system had all the virtues claimed for it. Not all large firms in Germany and the United States, of course, were in the hands of experts trained in science, technology or business. In those countries also the self-made man, the untaught business genius, made his mark, while at the other extreme the director who owed his place to nepotism was common enough. But there, and also in Japan, then in the early stages of industrialisation, it was becoming increasingly the practice for the administration of large firms to rest in the hands of men who had received a systematic train-

---

[48] Professor Postan refers to the small proportion of technicians 'promoted to directorships or top management in the United Kingdom' and quotes D. G. Clark, *The Industrial Manager*, Business Publications, 1966, and C. F. Carter and B. R. Williams, *Scientists in Industry*, Oxford University Press, 1959, in support. (M. M. Postan, *op. cit.*, p. 272.) In the large corporations, however, accountants are an exception to the generalisation in the text.

ing in disciplines related to their responsibilities. Just after the turn of the century, a leading German business man described to Sir William Ashley the kind of men normally sought for the boards of substantial companies and the education appropriate to them. A typical board should include, among others, a lawyer trained in a university law department, a technical expert from a Technischehochschule such as Charlottenburg, and one or two men who had received a systematic business training, which of course covered accountancy, in a Handelshochschule.[49] Amateurs from the public schools and with pass degrees from the universities, or promoted foremen, could not be expected to hold their own in competition with such highly trained professionals.

The cult of the amateur

The persistent belief in the merits of leaving high policy to the amateur was associated with the dominance of the classics in the university curriculum. For the majority of civil servants in the administrative class, classics formed the foundation and super-structure of their education. This was true of the governing class in general. The chief criticism that may be directed against the system was not that these men spent an excessive proportion of their university life in studies that were 'useless', for the distinction between 'useful' and 'useless' subjects is difficult to draw.[50] Whether one believes that 'learning Greek teaches Greek and nothing else, certainly not commonsense', or that those who have been taught to refer the great questions of civilised society to the oracles of Hellas are rendered immune against the malady of cultural chauvinism and the folly of extremes, the classics must always find an honoured place in Western education.[51] The English educational system was not open to criticism because it assigned a high place to the classics but simply because it left little room for anything else. Science and technology, in particular, were grossly neglected, a remarkable state of affairs when one considers the distinction of British scientists from the time of Bacon. This charge applies not only to the universities, but to English education as a whole.

[49] W. J. Ashley, *Commercial Education, op. cit.*, p. 65.
[50] The present writer is not so naive as to suppose that all modern subjects are 'useful' because they are modern. Professor J. K. Galbraith, it may be noted, regards most of modern economic theory as useless as a guide to contemporary economic developments!
[51] Cf. A. Toynbee, *op. cit.*, pp. 910–11.

The neglect is all the more surprising since as long ago as 1867 the alarm had been sounded about Britain's backwardness in these subjects. Dr Lyon Playfair of Edinburgh (a Scot, it should be noted) observed after a visit to the Paris Exhibition that

> 'our country had shown little inventiveness and made but little progress in the peaceful arts since 1862'. One cause, 'on which there was most unanimity of conviction', was that 'France, Prussia, Austria, Belgium and Switzerland possess good systems of industrial education for the masters and managers of factories and workshops and that Britain possesses none.'

'Technical education', he added, 'had given a great impulse to the industry of France.' He found that 'whenever anything excellent in French manufacture' struck the attention, the management of the establishment that produced it had usually been a pupil of the École Centrale des Arts et Manufactures.[52] About the same time it was noted that the great Polytechnic of Zurich drew its pupils from every European country except Britain, for no Englishman had come forward who could qualify for entrance.[53]

By this time the question of education in science had at last forced itself on the attention of the government. A Select Committee on Scientific Instruction reported in 1868 and the Devonshire Commission was appointed in 1872 to inquire into the scientific needs of the country. In 1881 the question of technical training was taken up by the Royal Commission on Technical Instruction, but the country had to wait until 1889 for the Technical Instruction Act which empowered the larger local authorities to organise technical education. There had, of course, been private initiatives such as that which led to the foundation

---

[52] *Schools Inquiry Commission: Report relative to Technical Education* (1867), quoted in W. H. B. Court, *op. cit.*, pp. 168–9.

[53] Professor Fleeming Jenkin, FRS, who held the Chair of Civil Engineering at University College London, before proceeding to a similar Chair at Edinburgh, during his evidence to the *Select Committee on Scientific Instruction*, which reported in July 1868, spoke of the Polytechnic at Zurich which had become a scientific university. This institution then had 600 students of whom half were foreigners. But there was no Englishman among them. 'I believe the reason is,' said Jenkin, 'that among the English the class of boys does not exist who could take these [entrance] examinations'. I am indebted to Professor Margaret Gowing for this information. Also, for information about scientific and technical education in Britain in the 19th century, D. S. L. Cardwell, *op. cit.*, p. 117 and *passim*.

of the Regent Street Polytechnic (1882). Training in science and technology had been introduced by a number of civic colleges, such as Owens College at Manchester (established in 1851) and Mason College at Birmingham (established in 1880).[54] There and at the London colleges, notably University College and Kings College, those subjects occupied a place of outstanding importance in the curriculum. But before the First World War they received far less attention in Britain than on the Continent. This showed itself in the shortage of men with a systematic training in technology and the sciences. When Lady Chorley's father joined Mather and Platt in the 1880s the engineering industry had little use for bright young men from the universities. Most firms preferred 'lads who had been through the works and had practical knowledge rather than theoretical knowledge.'[55] Until the 1890s the lack of men with a professional training in science forced the Department of Science and Art to employ officers of the Royal Engineers as school inspectors. The notable contribution of the Royal Military Academy to the supply of engineers and other technologists has seldom been adequately acknowledged. The Academy even exerted an influence on school education. At that time only a few public schools concerned themselves seriously with science, and the prominence given to the subject in at least one of them, Cheltenham (where it had an important place in the curriculum from the 1850s), can be explained by its links with the RMA.

The steel industry also cared little for scientific and technical training. Sheffield provided a good example of this attitude : '. . . What is quite clear is that in 1884 Sheffield industry did not want a Technical School enough to pay for it'.[56] Nor was there a marked improvement in this respect for the next 30 years. It has been estimated that, in the steel industry as a whole, fewer than 10 per cent of the leaders before the First World War had

[54] Eric W. Vincent and Percival Hinton, *The University of Birmingham: Its History and Significance*, Cornish, Birmingham, 1947, give a concise account of the evolution of a civic university from medical and science colleges.
[55] C. Erickson, *op. cit.*, p. 35n. The same attitude can still be found. A few years ago I talked with a young Japanese graduate in electrical engineering who had spent some months, as part of his training, in a power station in the Manchester area. He was astonished at the poor intellectual quality of the young Englishmen who were his fellow-trainees. They were pure empiricists, he said, uninterested in scientific principles, technicians, not engineers in embryo. Unfortunately, I was not able to get *their* opinion of *him*!
[56] A. W. Chapman, *The Story of a Modern University*, OUP, 1955, pp. 38–9.

received either a technical school training or a university education in science.[57]

The shortage of chemists and of chemical engineers,[58] to which attention had been called in 1886, had not been repaired by the time of the First World War when Britain found herself entirely dependent on Germany for aniline dyes. The ascendancy of Germany in the electrical and organic chemical industries has been ascribed to the receptivity of the managerial élite, the professionals in control of the large firms, to technological innovation, a receptivity which itself turned on certain institutional features of national life. Traditionally the Germans held university learning and science in great respect and, since the standards of technical education were very high, 'the links between the laboratory and factory were formed earlier and more easily among them' than in most other European societies.[59] Britain stood at the opposite extreme.

Britain lagged behind in business education

It was not only in the application of scientific knowledge to industry that Britain fell behind in the decades before 1914. The same was true of business education. The anti-intellectualist bias of British society, together with the prejudice against vocational education in the universities, was mainly responsible for Britain's long delay in introducing a system of training for the higher reaches of business comparable with that found among her commercial rivals.

In 1926 Ashley, a pioneer in establishing business education at British universities, emphasised the contrasts between his own country and both Continental countries and the United States. He concluded his survey of British commercial education in both government-aided and private institutions by asserting that, even by the time he was writing (1926), this education was

'second-rate, contributing less than it should to the production of routine clerkly efficiency and contributing little to the production of the higher qualities of business judgement'.[60]

Ashley's own Faculty of Commerce at Birmingham, founded on the insistence of Joseph Chamberlain, and similar Faculties and

[57] C. Erickson. *op. cit.*, p. 41.
[58] Not only of chemists: just before the 1914–18 war there were probably not more than 300 science students engaged in systematic post-graduate research in England and Wales. (Cardwell, *op. cit.*, p. 215.)
[59] M. M. Postan, *op. cit.*, p. 287.
[60] W. J. Ashley, *Commercial Education*, *op. cit.*, p. 56.

[45]

Departments established later at other places, received only modest support from the business community and for many years made little impact on British commercial and industrial management.

Business education in Germany ...

In Germany, on the other hand, from 1901 business education at university level was provided by a number of Handelshochschulen. By the First World War the Handelshochschule of Cologne, to take one instance, had over 500 matriculated students. Some of these colleges later achieved the status of universities. The older universities themselves introduced business studies. By the middle 1920s the students in the Handelshochschulen had reached nearly 5,000 and students of economics and allied subjects in all institutions of higher education some 11,000.[61] At that time there were probably fewer than 1,500 university students of economics and commerce in Britain.

In the United States, where business attracted a high proportion of the most able young men, business education was well developed. Its quality varied widely, reaching at the apex Harvard's Graduate School of Business Administration. By 1924 the enrolment in the departments of business administration and commerce in universities and colleges came to about 80,000. The study of business methods was also taken up in the American Schools of Engineering, which may explain why in the United States engineers were usually endowed with a keener appreciation of the economic side of their work than their typical British counterparts. Ashley's comment on the diffusion of business training in the United States is worth quoting, since his words by implication bring Britain's commercial deficiencies into high relief :

'In America business bulks more largely in men's thoughts than in an older country. The army and navy as careers hardly exist, the management of land is not associated with the existence of an aristocratic class and is entirely commercial; the older professions ... are more and more receding in relative importance; and the weight attached in Germany or France to the governmental service is not even conceivable. Hence it is that the movement for business training ... is now

[61] *Ibid.*, pp. 61–96.

quite certainly the largest of the waves passing over the American Universities.'[62]

This was the position in the middle 1920s, after several decades of development.

...and in Japan

High-grade vocational training was emphasised also in Japan's educational system from the time her Westernisation began. A college for business education was created as early as 1875, three years after the abolition of 'feudalism'. Initially it was a private foundation, but it later passed under the Ministry of Education and developed into the University of Commerce (now Hitotsubashi University). Several colleges modelled on the Handelshochschulen were established in the early 1900s, and by 1930 there were eleven of them, as well as three government universities which specialised in economics and commercial subjects. Between them these institutions, together with the economics and commerce departments at other universities, probably produced 4,000–5,000 graduates a year.

There were similar developments in technical education. The large firms already looked to these institutions for recruits for their technical and administrative staffs. In the 1920s it was unusual to meet an officer of the banks, industrial companies or merchant houses who had not been trained, in a college or university, in subjects appropriate to his duties. At that time, while the larger chemical and engineering firms in Britain were recruiting part of their technical staffs from the universities, few firms had any use for graduates in economics or commerce. The majority of the administrative staffs were recruited from the secondary schools and, although many of them supplemented their general education by evening studies at technical and commercial schools, they relied mainly on experience to teach them what they had to know.

Neglect of professional training to promote innovation

Now it is the contention of this *Paper* that the decline of Britain as an industrial and trading country had its roots in the failure of the governing class, as well as industrialists themselves, to realise, as early as their competitors, that the age of the professional in industrial management had dawned and, in

[62] *Ibid.*, pp. 101–2.

particular, to grasp that the future lay with men equipped by systematic training to promote technological innovation.[63] The chief blame must be assigned to what we now call the 'establishment' : political leaders, the Civil Service and those who sat on the boards of the chief industrial companies. They themselves were, of course, the victims of anachronistic institutions—the English class system and the educational arrangements associated with it.

Even when graduates in science and technology began to emerge from the universities, new and old, they found themselves in a world that often gave them a cold welcome and was incapable of appreciating their worth. Those in control of affairs, right up to the Second World War, being for the most part innocent of scientific knowledge themselves, could not make effective use of the expertise available to them. The politicians' attitude to science was for a long time that typified by Gladstone in his encounter with Faraday.

'The man of science tried in vain to explain some simple piece of apparatus to this fine flower of the parliamentary world. "But", said Mr Gladstone, "after all, what *good* is it?" "Why, sir," said Faraday, doing his best to bring things home to him, "presently you will be able to tax it." '[64]

There had been little advance in understanding even by the beginning of the new century. Of the politicians of that time, only A. J. Balfour and Lord Haldane[65] were perceptive enough to

---

63 A high proportion of Britain's industrial innovations before the First World War was attributable to foreign immigrants, e.g. Ludwig Mond, Charles Dreyfus, Hans Renold, William Siemens . . .

64 H. G. Wells, *The Outline of History*, George Newnes, 1921, Vol. 2, p. 663; Wells gave R. A. Gregory's *Discovery* as the source of this story. At the time of the encounter, Gladstone was Chancellor of the Exchequer.

65 Some sentences from a speech by Lord Haldane to the House of Lords in 1916 are worth quoting since they show that he at least was alive to the need in Britain for more scientific and technical training. 'On inquiry at a source on which reliance could be placed I found that there were only 1,500 trained chemists in the country altogether, and the reason was that we had not the means of encouragement to produce the business kind that was wanted. Our public schools do not aim at preparing an aptitude in the boys' minds for the study of chemistry : nor do our secondary schools; nor have we any trade continuation schools which stimulate the working man's son of exceptional talent to go on with this. Nor are universities equipped to produce men in these large numbers.' He went on to point out that 'four large German chemical firms which have played havoc with certain departments of our trade employ 1,000 highly trained chemists between them. These men were trained and produced by the great schools which exist there for that purpose'. (Sir Frederick Maurice, *The Life of Viscount Haldane of Cloan*, Faber & Faber, 1939, Vol. 2, pp. 30–2.)

grasp the importance of science to Britain's continued prosperity. The civil servants were crippled by their education and the environment in which they worked. Even the industrialists who employed scientists and technologists were seldom willing, or able, to make effective use of their talents. In an illuminating study of the European chemical industry, Professor P. M. Hohenberg has explained how it was that Britain, the pioneer in the development of the industry and the mother of many distinguished chemists, lost her lead to Germany and Switzerland before the end of the 19th century. The superiority of German and Swiss technical education is usually given as the reason, and this was certainly an important factor. But the crucial cause was the failure of British firms to admit chemists and other scientists to a share in policy-making. In Germany chemists sat as a matter of course on the boards of directors; in Britain their counterparts played a subordinate role as advisers.[66] In Germany the expert was found at the centre of the decision-making process; in Britain his exclusion meant that the last word was with the amateurs. This may well provide the clue to many failures in British projects that made a promising start. The same kind of criticism could also be levelled against management in some of the large engineering firms.

Role of the technical expert

Now it is not suggested that policy-making should be vested entirely in technical experts who are not always alert to the economic and social aspects of the choices they have to make. From the time of Telford, who persuaded the government to build at uncontrollable expense the almost wholly useless Caledonian Canal,[67] down to the aeronautical advisers who induced the government to embark on the construction of Concorde, there have been many examples that demonstrate the truth of Rothschild's warning:

'There are three roads to ruin, women, gambling and engineers; the first two are the more agreeable, but the last is the surest.'[68]

[66] P. M. Hohenberg, *Chemicals in Western Europe, 1850–1914*, North-Holland Publishing Co., 1967, Chap. 3.
[67] A. J. Youngson, *After the Forty-Five*, Edinburgh University Press, 1973, is a brilliant study of 'regional policy' as applied to Scotland 200 years ago.
[68] 'Il y a trois manières de se ruiner, disait le grand Rothschild: le jeu, les femmes et les ingénieurs. Les deux premières sont plus agréables ... mais la dernière est plus sure.' (A. Detoeuf, *Propos de O. L. Barenton, Confiseur*, Editions du Tamboutinaire, Paris, 1958.)

Yet, while it is rash to leave decisions on large projects entirely to technical experts, it is equally improvident to *exclude* them from a powerful influence in determining what should be done. To be effective, moreover, the expert must be of the company of decision-makers, not a subordinate adviser. When complicated technical questions have to be decided, only the expert is competent to make an informed judgement among alternatives. If he is to be over-ruled on economic or other grounds (and this may often be necessary), he must at least participate in the debate as a member of the team of decision-makers. And when, as sometimes happens, the expert is a man of wide and diversified experience which has obliged him to face harsh economic truth, he may turn out to be the ideal leader.[69] Britain's industrial progress was gravely hindered by the strong prejudice, in government and many branches of industry itself, against the expert, a prejudice rooted in social and educational tradition, a prejudice which carried into a technological age the practices and attitudes of mind inherited from a pre-scientific time.

It is not fanciful to see an analogy between Britain at the apogee of her power and Imperial China. The mandarins, selected by competitive examinations in the classics, were contemptuous of science and condemned scientific inquiry as impious. The rules laid down by Confucius for the conduct of gentlemen in positions of authority were adequate guides in every situation in life. But the time came when the Chinese rulers lost the Mandate of Heaven.

IV. LATE ADAPTATION TO CHANGE

After the First World War it seemed that Britain might shrug off the incubus of the past and strike out along new paths. At the universities, both new and old, there was a wide extension of subjects and faculties, and science and technology rose in esteem.

[69] What can be achieved when scientists and technologists of exceptional quality are given their head has been depicted by Professor Margaret Gowing in her work on the successful British atomic energy project just after the Second World War. Sir John Cockroft, Sir Christopher Hinton and Sir William Penney not only supplied the expert knowledge and the imagination demanded for the solution of novel and formidable scientific and technological problems; they also showed superb skill as entrepreneurs and organisers, and they even bent the bureaucratic machine to their service. (Margaret Gowing, *Independence and Deterrence: Britain and Atomic Energy, 1945-1952*, Macmillan, 2 vols., 1964.)

The government, shaken by wartime evidence of the country's technical deficiencies, began to concern itself with scientific research. The newer industries recruited increasing numbers of graduates in science and technology. Some of the leading firms enlarged their research activities and began to co-operate in research through the joint bodies set up in association with the newly-formed Department of Industrial and Scientific Research. A few enlightened industrialists addressed themselves to the problem of improving management in Britain, and the Management Research Group movement came into being, inspired by the energy and imagination of Seebohm Rowntree. During the 1920s and 1930s many of the more progressive firms participated in these groups and the notion that there was advantage in subjecting managerial practices to scientific scrutiny spread.

Tardy spread of professionalism in management

Yet it could not be claimed that the professionalisation of management had advanced as far in England as among her leading rivals, and British industry failed conspicuously to respond to the challenge of international competition. As the staple industries came under pressure from foreigners, both government and industry adopted a defensive posture. It still seemed inconceivable that Britain's economy should not continue to rest on the staple exporting industries associated with her rise to supremacy. So to sustain them became a major part of economic policy, especially after the onset of the world depression of 1929. Schemes for the alleviation of the lot of the old staples proceeded from government, academics (though not often from economists) and industrialists themselves. Frequently they required the suppression of competition by cartelisation or combination. Sometimes restrictive practices were enforced on reluctant firms by the government. Measures for strengthening the the competitive power of associated manufacturers in the home market multiplied after the introduction of a general protective tariff in 1932. The tariff was supplemented in some industries (e.g. steel) by quantitative restrictions on imports, and several commercial treaties provided for discrimination in favour of British exports of coal and textiles in return for concessions to certain foreign suppliers to Britain. The suppression of, or control over, competition was extended to transport, agriculture and other non-factory trades, and in all of them the defence of the established producers was the main objective. This policy fostered the worst instincts among business men. There were, of course, some resourceful industrialists who introduced new lines of production and innovations in processes. But the chief effect of the government's intervention between the wars was to defend the failures rather than to encourage the enterprising.

Britain was not, of course, the only country to adopt defensive measures of the type described during the 1930s. But it may be argued that, with such a high proportion of her industry concentrated in the older branches of manufacture and with her poor showing in the newer industries, any restrictions that impeded the mobility of resources and served to maintain the *status quo* were particularly damaging to her.

The West Midlands: lessons unheeded

The various industrial regions made different responses to the challenge of the period. If the government had taken heed of the experience of one of them, British industry might today have been in better shape. This was the West Midlands which, in the course of its recent history, had effected a complete transformation of its industrial structure and, in consequence, had maintained its prosperity.

In the 1870s this region was specialised to coal-mining, ironmaking, hardware, guns, jewellery, buttons and brassfoundry. The last four trades were the staples of Birmingham itself. Under the influence of outside competition and changes in markets and technical methods, these industries decayed, but the region maintained, and indeed appreciably increased, its prosperity by turning to a group of new industries : cycles, motor-cars, electrical apparatus, leather goods, confectionery and other manufactures that served new markets.

A study of this experience led the present writer to propose in 1929 :

'... the success of Birmingham and District in effecting a fundamental change in the nature of its industrial interests points to the conclusion that, for the entire country, policy should be directed towards speeding up the inevitable transformation and towards easing the process of transition, rather than towards supporting by artificial means the decaying members of the industrial structure.'[70]

[70] G. C. Allen, *The Industrial Development of Birmingham and the Black Country, 1860–1927*, Allen & Unwin, 1929, p. 454. The author apologises for quoting himself and promises not to do it again.

As we have shown, this lesson went unheeded. In consequence, while Britain participated in the development of such trades as motor manufacture, electrical goods and rayon, she failed to gain a rank in the new markets equivalent to that she once held in markets for her old staples. An inquiry into the exports of three leading countries showed that in the inter-war years Britain's export specialisation was on goods in which world trade had risen very little, whereas American exports consisted predominantly of goods in which world trade was expanding rapidly.[71] It was the relative stagnation of Britain in the newer trades, even more than the decline of her old industries, that was the chief symptom of her loss of industrial leadership.

Government policies frustrated adaptation to change

Britain's performance, as judged by her rate of growth, was certainly better in the inter-war years than in the period immediately before the First World War, despite the heavy chronic unemployment and the dip in production during the Great Depression of 1930–33. But it is clear that she lacked the resilience necessary for the major structural adjustments that her circumstances required. In part the fault lay with those in control of industry, but the bias of government policy in both political parties towards maintaining the *status quo* was also to blame.

During the Second World War the government assumed the direction of the economy and the heads of firms were, to a large extent, transformed into functionaries administering resources in accordance with official rules. It became the practice for trade associations or other representative bodies to work with the civil servants in the control of prices, production and manpower. The result was that when, towards the end of the war, the government began to discuss with industry plans for reconstruction, it found that most of the firms were thinking in terms of preserving wartime forms of organisation or of a re-affirmation of the restrictionism of the 1930s.

By this time, however, the government had had second thoughts about the suppression of competition, for it had realised that measures to maintain the 'full employment' to which it had committed itself were likely, in conditions of monopoly and restrictions, to lead to higher prices rather than to increased production and employment. So it adopted a posture of mild hostility towards monopoly and restrictive practices, to the

---

[71] A. J. Brown, *Applied Economics*, Library of Economics, 1947, p. 200.

[53]

indignation of the business men brought up in the pre-war era. Firms that became subject to inquiries under the Monopolies and Restrictive Practices Act (1948) remonstrated, very reasonably, that the government now appeared to be blaming them for employing practices of a kind which had received warm official encouragement before 1939. It took them some time to grasp why conduct considered virtuous before the war should be condemned as contrary to the public interest in the 1950s. Those with a sense of irony observed that the civil servants of the department chiefly responsible for administering the anti-monopoly policy comprised some officials who, a short time before, had fostered the restrictions.

Industry's slow acceptance of post-war anti-monopoly policy

The British business world eventually acquiesced in the monopoly policy which gathered force and widened its scope as time went on. There is evidence to show that, although the policy probably did little or nothing to halt the trend towards monopolies of scale—a world-wide phenomenon—the measures for curbing restrictive practices exerted by the 1960s a significant effect in stimulating competition in a wide range of industries.[72] In particular, the attack on resale price maintenance was pursued after 1964, the year of the Resale Prices Act, with more determination in Britain than in most other countries. On the other hand, in the immediate post-war years British enterprise was at a disadvantage in one respect compared with that of several of her chief competitors. In the defeated countries there was a 'purge' of politicians, officials and administrators who had held power in government and economic life and who were now regarded as the architects of ruin. In Japan, for instance, the dissolution of the *Zaibatsu* (the great conglomerates) in the late 1940s confirmed the transference of authority from the former industrial leaders. Much the same happened in West Germany. In France and Belgium many of those formerly in control of affairs were ousted because of their alleged collaboration with the enemy during the period of occupation. So among these competitors of Britain young men moved into the seats of power. They breathed a new air of freedom. They set out with zest to create a new industrial order; and the resurgence of those countries owes not a little to that determination. Britain, alas, both in government

---

[72] D. Swann, D. P. O'Brien, W. P. J. Maunder and W. S. Howe, *Competition in British Industry*, Allen & Unwin, 1974, Chap. 4.

and industry, was stuck with the leaders she already had, men who had been brought up in the restrictionist pre-war years. The dead hand of the past weighed down her enterprise in the critical years of reconstruction. The charm of continuity is seductive but emasculating.

V. THE PRESENT DAY: BRITAIN STILL LAGGING

Now it may be objected that most of these criticisms relate to a period long past and that by the middle 1970s they applied only to a small and diminishing sector of industry. The dominion of the pre-war leaders was short and by the end of the 1950s new men had moved into positions of authority. Management had become more highly professionalised. The sources of recruitment to its ranks had been augmented. Large firms had become accustomed to engage university graduates, not only those trained in science and technology, but also men with degrees in the arts and the social sciences for administrative work. In the 1960s Britain was at long last persuaded of the merits of a systematic academic training in business studies both at the graduate and post-graduate level.

British industry still failing to attract graduates and professionals
Even so, in comparison with other industrial countries, industry in Britain has not attracted a high proportion of the country's first-rate ability.[73] The inclination of the best graduates is still to prefer an academic career, research, the Civil Service or the professions to jobs in industry.[74] The mentors of the young must bear a share of the responsibility for this choice. They have been disposed to deflect their most promising pupils from employment in business to what they regard as worthier activities. Of this disposition Professor H. S. Ferns gave an illuminating example in a recent letter to *The Times*. At an examiners' meeting in the Faculty of Commerce at the University of Birmingham

[73] Is it fanciful to ascribe some part of the City's success as a producer of income and an exporter of services to its ability to attract a good deal of high-grade talent from the universities?

[74] They receive powerful incentive from the higher starting salaries now generally offered by central and local government. (Report by the Central Services Unit of the university careers services, *Daily Telegraph*, 11 December 1975.)

the examiners were debating the classification of a rather stupid young man :

> 'One of the lecturers, now a Professor at Cambridge, burst out "Give him a third and let him be a business man!"'

This attitude explains a lot of what is wrong with the British economy.[75] Some blame also attaches to employers. I recall an occasion when the high executives of firms in the engineering industry were complaining of the preference of graduates for work in their research departments and of their reluctance to take jobs on the production side of the industry.[76] My suggestion that a solution should be found by differential salary scales was dismissed as quite impracticable. The outlook for private enterprise is indeed bleak if employers reject the pricing system as a means for achieving a desired allocation of resources.

Persisting cult of the amateur

Despite the increasing professionalisation of management, the employment of highly trained scientists and technologists by many large businesses, and the substantial expenditure, public and private, on industrial and scientific research, the gap between Britain and her chief competitors in all but the last-named activity has remained. Foreigners are still surprised to discover how often their British counterparts lack a systematic training for the specific tasks they have to perform. Ezra Pound's description of England as 'a country in love with amateurs' has not yet been outmoded.[77] Britain in the 1970s still trailed behind her competitors in making profitable use of scientists and

---

[75] Letter in *The Times* (Business News), February, 1974.

[76] On this point the comment of the *Committee on the Productivity of the National Aircraft Effort* is illuminating (para. 334): 'Until very recently production has been regarded with some disdain by graduate engineers entering industry and by the senior management of many companies. They have seen production control as a routine, clerical activity demanding dogged application and the processing of large quantities of paper rather than as a task requiring bright new ideas. Consequently graduate engineers entering industry in this country have shown a marked preference for jobs in the design and development departments. Managements have done little to dispel this impression perhaps because they tend to be composed of people who have risen mainly through the design and development departments. It is an irrational attitude, however, because production is the end-result from which profits are made and investment in R & D recovered. The Americans have been quick to see these problems, but British firms have been slower to improve the status of production management staff and hence have experienced a shortage of people of the right calibre.'

[77] Michael Reck, *Ezra Pound: A Close-up*, Rupert Hart-Davis, 1968, p. 14.

technologists. When the Department of Scientific and Industrial Research some fifteen years ago inquired into the condition of the shipbuilding industry they found a wide disparity between Britain and West Germany (and some others) in the employment of graduate engineers.

Institutions and habits of mind, once firmly rooted, are not easy to displace in the absence of calamity or violent upheaval. The men in control of industry and government in the early years of the century tended to choose successors of their own stamp. In spite of the spread of science teaching and other modern studies in the schools, the development of new universities with a bias to science and technology, and the outstanding scientific discoveries in them, in the London colleges and in the famous laboratories of the older universities, the men who held the reins of power for most of the last half-century were brought up in the old tradition. Their influence remains powerful in our own day.

The politician's nostalgia

Mr Harold Macmillan (to quote again from his recent article in *The Times*) has voiced his regret (which many share) at the presence in Oxford of

> 'those no doubt essential but somehow discordant temples dedicated to science and technology', and he harks back to the days when 'there were happily no industries'

to mar the city's charms. Yet Mr Macmillan held high office throughout the 1950s and was Prime Minister until a decade and a half ago. He it was who spoke with authority of a 'wind of change' and of the British people's unprecedented prosperity ('you've never had it so good!'). Yet those temples and industries which were accepted with such reluctance were the main sources of such improved welfare as the British have enjoyed. They would have done still more for the people's standard of living if the energies of the country's leaders had been directed towards creating an environment favourable to their enhancement.

The civil servants' shortcomings

The Civil Service, for its part, has not been equipped to handle the problems of a technological age. Even today, although the sources of recruitment have been much extended, and economists and other social scientists are numbered among the administrative trainees, hardly any recruits have been trained in science and technology. This would not have mattered if it had not been for the government's increasing participation in industrial affairs. At a time when vast sums of public money have been committed to investment, both in new projects and in old-established industries, those who have taken the decisions have lacked the intimate acquaintance with industrial, scientific and technological matters that is a condition of prudent judgement. That the competence of the authorities in this sphere has been a pretence has been demonstrated by the long series of costly mistakes.[78] In the 1960s those who had little or no knowledge of industry set out to 'plan' it, with consequences as derisory as they were predictable. The fatuity of this policy and of the means devised for executing it have been eloquently exposed by an industrialist who was one of its victims,[79] but consistent failure does not seem to have deterred the authorities from further experiments of the same kind.

> '. . . the burnt Fool's bandaged finger goes
> wabbling back to the Fire'.

'Planning': the fallacious comparison with France and Japan

Those who support some form of planning point to the successful outcome of the close association of government with industry in policy-making procedures in Japan and France. But in those countries, as already shown, the authorities have joined with industry in promoting conditions favourable to economic growth, which has been a primary national objective, consistently pursued. In Britain it has seemed to business men that industrial progress has been assigned a low place in the official list of priorities, and that considerations of efficiency are held in scant regard by policy-makers. It is not suggested here, of course, that efficiency should always command policy in a civilised society, but only that countries in which it stands high in the order of preference are those where a rapid rate of growth is likely to be achieved. The rejection of private capitalism by many of Britain's leading politicians and the fiscal burdens and restrictions imposed by a succession of post-war governments have robbed manufacturers of the confidence upon which high endeavour must largely

---

[78] It may be argued that the very fact that the Civil Service has to work within parliamentary rules and procedures inevitably increases the difficulty (and the cost) of administration in the industrial and commercial sphere.

[79] F. S. (now Sir Frank) McFadzean, a managing director of Shell, in *Galbraith and the Planners*, University of Strathclyde, 1968.

depend. The result is that, even on the occasions when government has set out to stimulate the growth of production (as in the days of the Department of Economic Affairs (DEA)), business men have been in sceptical mood and have been grudging in their co-operation. To them it seemed that the civil servants, no less than the politicians, had little understanding of, and less sympathy with, their problems. So many of the conditions needed for the successful association of government and industry in formulating and executing sensible economic policies were absent.

It is instructive to compare the sceptical response of the British industrialists to the various national plans of the 1960s with that of their Japanese counterparts. When in 1960 the Japanese government announced its 'income doubling' plan for the next decade, the response was a surge of private investment and a sharp acceleration in the rate of production. Previous experience had given the Japanese industrialist confidence that he could rely on his government to create the conditions necessary to achieve its stated aim. In consequence, the Japanese rate of growth during the 1960s turned out to be far higher than had been planned, whereas the British plans met the usual fate that attends efforts that are half-hearted.

The experiences of that part of the economy that is entirely subject to planning have served to increase the distrust on the part of the business community for the capacity of government to plan the rest. In the operation of the nationalised industries, the main faults are not to be found in management, which has sometimes been of high quality, but in the interference of Ministers with the processes of price-making, investment and location. Usually that interference has been designed to promote some political or social objective, such as holding down prices at uneconomic levels or diverting new investment to areas of high unemployment, even if costs of manufacture or supply were raised considerably in consequence. From time to time governments have declared that they will allow the nationalised industries to be guided by the 'commercial principle', but they can be counted on, sooner or later, to lapse from this virtuous resolve.

Those who find difficulties in coping with the major problems of life occupy themselves with trivialities. In the same way, post-war governments, unwilling to face the realities of Britain's deteriorating economy, have been inclined to fill their days with inessential, secondary or irrelevant activities. Their preoccupation with forms of organisation and the machinery of administration provides an outstanding example. Instead of concentrating on the large issues of economic policy, they have found it easier to busy themselves with modifications in administrative arrangements. All the nationalised industries have been the frequent victims of this manoeuvre. The same applies to the government departments themselves. The DEA, the Ministry of Technology and some others have come and gone; even the venerable Board of Trade and its offspring, the Ministry of Labour, have been replaced by departments with other names, or have been merged, without any obvious improvement in the efficiency of the government's economic management.

British governments since the war are also open to criticism for their lack of foresight in the conduct of international economic policy. The first post-war Labour government kept Britain out of the Coal and Steel Community, and the Conservative government under Mr Eden refused to participate in the EEC in its formative stages and in the making of the Treaty of Rome. Consequently, in the period of exceptionally rapid economic growth in the world economy, British industry continued to direct its attention mainly to the slow-growing Commonwealth markets rather than towards the faster-growing European markets. When, ultimately and inevitably, Britain joined the Community she had to accept the rules already drawn up by the well-established members, although some of those rules placed her at a disadvantage. However, in mitigation one must admit that the government's policy in this field reflected the attitude of the British people who for many years remained reluctant to accept the (for them) disagreeable changes of the post-war world.

There are some who argue, though not with complete justification, that many of the faults that are commonly ascribed to Ministers and civil servants are simply the result of their obedience to democratic pressures. It is an old problem.

'... we are confronted by the difficulty of an Executive summoned to all-pervading duties, but with agents who receive little popular support. The public demands inspection, but too often denounces the inspectors; the public demands regulations, but chafes at the red tape employed in carrying them out; ... it demands organisations which require the appointment of vast numbers of clerks, yet the deficiencies of govern-

[60]

ment clerks and the expense of their salaries and pensions furnish endless food for popular declamation.'

These were the words of Viscount Goschen in *1883*![80]

Government ignorance of conditions for industrial efficiency

British industry, so it has been suggested, has long suffered from the failure of government to understand its problems and from the presumption that, however heavily burdened or neglected, it could be relied on to supply the income necessary for the pursuit of other national ambitions. In recent years, just when management was becoming more highly professionalised, the relations between industry and government deteriorated. Those who should have been partners in the development of the economy found themselves at cross-purposes and the antagonism has deepened with the passage of years, with disastrous effects on entrepreneurial morale. When the relationship in Britain is compared with that between government and industry in many other countries, there is no wonder that Britain has done badly. To this handicap to economic progress one must add the condition of industrial relations in which the British have shown themselves to be conspicuously inept during the last 20 years. Organised labour, government and industry have all been pulling different ways. It is difficult to see how an economy can flourish in the face of such animosity among those who should be partners.

The 'British Disease' worsened by industrial relations

An analysis of the problem of industrial relations in its historical and contemporary aspects is necessarily part of a study of the 'British Disease'. In the substantial part of industry which is composed of small and medium-sized firms, relations between employers and workers have probably been as harmonious as in any country. But in many of the large-scale industries, including those in the public sector, labour troubles have been endemic.

The loss to production that resulted from bad industrial relations cannot in any period be judged solely by figures of stoppages and the number of days lost by disputes of all kinds, although the upward trend in the last decade is a symptom of deterioration. Even more damage to the economy has been inflicted by trade-union restrictions on the efficient operation of labour-saving plant, obstruction which in some trades has led to chronic over-

80 'Laissez-Faire and Government Interference', in *Essays and Addresses on Economic Questions*, pp. 313–14.

manning and in others has deterred firms from investing in new equipment. Examples can be found in a wide range of industries in recent years. The new Seaforth grain terminal remained idle for two years through a dispute about manning; the introduction of the high-speed train in which British Rail had invested heavily has been delayed through the objections of train drivers to the conditions proposed; much the same can be said of the troubles in the coming into service of new aircraft, such as the TriStar. Capital has run to waste through the dockers' resistance to containerisation; costs in printing have been kept artificially high because of disputes about conditions of work and manning; new, efficient equipment at man-made fibres plants has been kept idle for the same reason; costly, highly productive blast furnaces have remained unused because of the failure of management and the unions to reach agreement about wages to be paid for their operation. At the same time the mood of the workers in many factories has been such as to engage a high proportion of the energies of middle management simply in keeping the men at work. Inter-union quarrels on demarcation and jurisdiction have been responsible for many stoppages of work. In some of the major industries—motor-cars, coal-mining, shipbuilding, printing, railway transport and the docks—the record is lamentable and has become worse in recent years than it was in the 1950s. There are traditions and experience of conciliation and arbitration that in some trades extend back for a century or more, indeed long before wage-bargaining machinery was created by the state. But these procedures seem to have worked less smoothly during the last decade.

Industrial harmony foiled by craft unions

Many hopeful innovations in industrial relations have come to grief. Towards the end of the First World War the Whitley Committee's recommendations were given the force of law, and the Whitley Councils and Committees established in consequence seemed to open the way to employer-worker collaboration in the solution of common problems. The trend towards industrial unionism after the war promised to go far in reducing demarcation disputes among unions and in some minds foreshadowed worker participation in management. In the Second World War unions and management co-operated in solving the problems of war production and this experience again inspired hopes of future harmony. But these prospects were illusory. Industrial unionism failed in the face of the determined opposition of the well-entrenched craft unions, and organised labour lost any enthusiasm it may have possessed for workers' participation, preferring to take up the stance of a 'permanent' opposition to the management.[81]

When, after the Second World War, the arrival of the 'welfare state' and the commitment of government to a policy of full employment strengthened the unions, it was unfortunate that this power was held by a large number of separate organisations each fighting for its own hand. This structure had been inherited from the past. Craft unions, occupational unions, general workers' unions and industrial unions had developed at different periods and have continued to exist side by side, often in rivalry with one another. There were some far-sighted trade union leaders who realised that the maintenance of this obsolete structure, and the methods of negotiation that went with it, would be detrimental to productivity and so in the long run to the welfare of the workers. Sir Alan Birch argued that the TUC should become an instrument for close integration in the field of wage-bargaining so that 'competing and sometimes irreconcilable claims' by individual unions could be eliminated.[82] In some large firms joint negotiating machinery was devised for handling their industrial relations as a whole, and in the operation of this machinery representatives of all the unions concerned took part. But efforts such as these were sometimes defeated by the revolt of the workers on the shop floor against agreements reached centrally. Sir Alan Birch's ambitions for the TUC had little chance of success in an atmosphere of inter-union suspicion and a jealous regard for autonomy on the part of the various organisations. This area of national life, like so many others, was flawed by humbug. Just as government has affected an expertise in industrial affairs that it does not possess, so the TUC has deluded the public by a pretence of authority over individual unions which they by their actions have often repudiated.

Trade unions more damaging in Britain than in other countries

All other industrial countries have suffered from labour troubles since the war, but it is in Britain that they seem to have exerted the most damaging effect on production and so on living

81 H. R. G. Greaves, *Democratic Participation and Public Enterprise*, Athlone Press, 1964, p. 14.
82 Sir Alan Birch, *Structure of British Trade Union Movement*, Manchester Statistical Society, 1957, pp. 23–4.

standards. Several countries have been successful in promoting co-operation between management and workers, whereas in many of the major British industries the achievements in this sphere have been narrowly limited.

In West Germany, where Works Councils have a long history, employees have joined with their employers in seeking more efficiency and, through their representation on the Aufsichtsräte, share responsibility for the policy of the individual companies.

In Japan the trade unions were created from nothing after the war within a framework of labour laws introduced by the Occupation Authority. During the years that followed a system of industrial relations grew up that proved to be wholly in accord with the needs of a progressive, technologically-advanced industrial society. The chief features of the system were the organisation of workers in 'enterprise unions', composed of all 'established' workers in particular firms, a guarantee of permanent employment to such workers, the determination of wages chiefly by reference to age and seniority and their supplementation by bi-annual bonuses that vary with the firm's profits. The interests of the 'two sides' of industry thus became closely linked and the dangers to productivity of inter-union rivalries and of resistance to technical changes were eliminated. Moreover, the Japanese system of management, though hierarchical in form, offered considerable scope for participation on the part of different grades of employees.

The contrasting attitudes of British and Japanese workers have been clearly demonstrated by Professor Ronald Dore. He tells us that if a Japanese worker is asked what he does, he is likely to reply, first of all, that he is an employee of Hitachi or Matsushita or whatever his firm is. His British counterpart will almost certainly say that he is a fitter or an electrician. His loyalties are to his occupational group, not to his employer.[83] The distinction between 'them' and 'us' is much sharper in Britain than in Japan.

Marx, Galbraith, Schumpeter and capitalist conflict

It is generally believed that the Japanese system has been shaped by social attitudes and traditions that have come down from ancient times (such as the elevation of duties above rights) but this cannot provide the whole explanation. In the early days of Japanese industrialism, relations between employers and workers

[83] *British Factory, Japanese Factory*, Allen & Unwin, 1973, especially Chaps. 8 and 9.

in the large firms closely resembled those in Britain. Labour turnover was high and the sense of a common purpose was absent. Subsequently, Japan chose the path of harmony surprising to those who believe, with Marx or Galbraith, in the theory of convergent social evolution. It might also have surprised Schumpeter, a more perceptive observer of social trends. According to him, modern industrialism, by reason of its very success in raising standards and expectations, was giving birth to attitudes of mind and claims among workers that were incompatible with the continuing success of the system.[84] Yet the conflicts he foresaw are evidently not inevitable, as is shown by the experience of many advanced countries in recent years, e.g. West Germany, Austria, Switzerland, Sweden and Japan. All these countries have devised institutions and systems of relations that have enabled them to avoid, so far, the predicted collision. It has been left to Britain, by repute the home of compromise and tolerance, to demonstrate that the theory is plausible.

Why more conflict in Britain than in other countries?

What is the explanation? Inflation has undoubtedly been responsible for much of the disorder in industrial relations. But inflation has afflicted in greater or less degree all countries in the post-war period. Though everywhere socially disruptive, its consequences have been less damaging to Britain's competitors than to herself. Other causes must have been operative. It is, of course, to be expected that the debate about distributional shares in a period of inflation will be less acrimonious in countries where the GNP is rising rapidly than in countries of low economic growth. But bad industrial relations are as much the cause as the consequence of economic stagnation. So one must look elsewhere. In industrial relations as in other parts of her national life, Britain is the victim of her past. For her there was not, as in most countries in modern times, any sharp break in her historical experience; she could boast of the good fortune of a land 'where freedom slowly broadens down from precedent to precedent'. Institutions and attitudes that were the product of past times persisted, modified but substantially unchanged, long after they had served their purpose. Some of them became a positive hindrance to progress. The effects of this continuity on the quality of leadership in industry and government have been described.

[84] J. A. Schumpeter, *Capitalism, Socialism and Democracy*, Unwin University Books (12th Impression, 1970), Chaps. 14 and 23.

Similarly, a trade-union structure built up in response to conditions in the 19th century has retained sufficient of its former identity to obstruct the birth of a more rational and appropriate system of industrial relations such as appeared in several countries after the Second World War.

The obsolete structure itself, and those who have striven to preserve it, are much to blame. But there are other causes, too. Management itself has done little to change the posture of confrontation inherited from the old days. During the 19th century there were enlightened employers who had the welfare of their workers at heart and whose relations with them were genial. Experiments in co-partnership have a long history and in recent times works councils and committees have been set up by forward-looking firms for the joint discussion of common problems as well as of disputes. But the area covered by such arrangements has always been narrowly limited. Most firms showed little enthusiasm for them and the trade unions were suspicious because they feared their members' loyalty to their class group might be weakened by such schemes. Only during the Second World War, in the face of a common enemy, was co-operation wholehearted and widespread. Then the British enjoyed the same unity that the defeated nations found in their task of recovery from the ruins of war. One is thus led back to institutions, attitudes and the challenges presented to societies, in order to explain these contrasts.

Management's attitude to industrial relations

In Britain management was for the most part slow in coming to terms with the new social temper. Many firms were not persuaded of the need for change; for them industrial relations were not a major pre-occupation of management until trouble came. The author has the firm impression that differences among firms in the same industry in the success with which they deal with their labour problems may often be ascribed to managerial priorities; firms where a senior director is in charge of industrial relations have been, so it seems, less prone to labour troubles than those where management is indifferent.

Finally, if one attempts to explain Britain's bad record in comparison with that of several of her rivals, one cannot avoid bringing her class structure into the account. Despite all the social changes of the post-war period, the vestigial remains of the old system still affect profoundly the relations between the two sides of industry with mischievous consequences for mutual understanding and ease of communication. In other countries also there are of course deep social and political cleavages, but they do not seem to be of the kind that have hampered economic progress. In some societies it is possible for people to hold to different standards of value and yet to respect each other's interests.

Class divisions dramatised

Despite the 'embourgeoisement' of a substantial part of the working class, the divisions in society remain as real as they are numerous and subtle. Nor are there simply 'two nations'; there are dozens. The lack of sympathy between different groups in British society has been brilliantly depicted by Professor Gowing in her description of the relations between the officers of HMS *Campania* and the group of scientists whom they were taking to the Monte Bello islands for the first British nuclear explosion. These two groups of dedicated, intelligent and dutiful men, all experts in their callings, were thrown together for the duration of a long voyage. Neither side was able to understand the quality of the other; their different education, upbringing and standards of behaviour kept them apart. 'The impact of two different worlds—the conservative, traditional and highly disciplined Navy and the informal, individualist "boffins"—was sharp'.[85] The formalities of naval conduct and ritual were derided by the scientists who, in flouting those conventions, earned the contempt and dislike of the officers.

If this lack of mutual understanding exists among members of the élite, how much wider is the gap between 'them' and 'us' in industry? Several factors have combined to produce this social disunity. Even some of the measures designed to alleviate the condition of the poorer members of the community are found among them. For instance, the housing schemes of the local authorities, which have helped to improve material well-being, have led to the creation of one-class localities the inhabitants of which are deprived of easy access to people in other groups. It may also be suggested that the divisive system of education must bear some share of responsibility. All countries, of course, must make provision for training an élite, but England is unique in possessing two entirely distinct systems of education from childhood upwards. Nowhere else are the children from different

[85] Margaret Gowing, *Independence and Deterrence: Britain and Atomic Strategy 1945–55*, Macmillan, Vol. 2, 1964, p. 486.

social groups kept so rigidly apart throughout their school life. Undoubtedly this characteristic of the educational system has been strongly influenced by the traditional British belief in the presiding importance of 'degree',[86] a belief that is still to be found at all levels of society. Here one can find a significant contrast between the British class system and the élitism of certain Continental countries, notably modern France. The former, as it affects both education and the ordering of affairs in general, rests on status, the latter increasingly on performance.

Contrast with Japanese education and social attitudes

The author noted, when he first visited Japan in the 1920s, that although it did not then claim to be democratic, children from all classes attended the same primary schools. A Japanese friend was surprised that I should have found this a matter for remark. Though he was well-to-do, he thought it natural that the people who were now his servants and the local farm workers should have attended the same primary school as he.[87] It seemed to me at the time, and since, that the common experience provided in early years by such an education added much to the sense of community and the uniform standard of manners that the nation possessed, and so was a source of strength to it in difficult times. Recently the high executive of a large foreign company who had spent some years in London mentioned to the author the surprise he felt as it dawned on him that, in an allegedly Socialist Britain, a very high proportion of the leading positions in public affairs was held by an exclusive group educated at a few privileged schools. He asked: 'Was it possible that the narrow educational basis of British leadership provided part of the explanation for her social troubles and for her stagnant economy?'

It is easier to detect weaknesses in the British educational system than to devise remedies. To enforce uniformity on a reluctant minority would probably do more harm than good and would certainly affront the widely-held convictions that parents have a right to choose the type of education for their children and that policy should be directed towards increasing

[86] That is, status; Shakespeare gave expression to this belief in a famous passage in *Troilus and Cressida*, Act I, Scene II.
[87] Contrast this attitude with that of a Labour Peer (and one-time Labour Minister) a few years ago. When criticised for having sent his son to Eton, he is reported to have replied that it was reasonable for him to make this choice since it ensured his son would be educated among those with whom he would consort in later life.

[68]

their ability to exercise that right. Some of the 'reforms' now in train are likely to make the system even more divisive than it is. For instance, the abolition of the grammar schools, and the removal of state support from the direct-grant schools, are likely to increase social polarisation by inducing more parents to send their children to independent schools.

The author does not pretend to offer any solution for the problem of how educational divisiveness in Britain can be modified without impairing individual freedom of choice and standards of educational excellence. But the difficulty of finding a solution of this intricate problem does not disturb the conclusion that, in this province of national life, as in others, certain British institutions and attitudes, whatever their merits *sub specie aeternitatis*, are incompatible with the needs of a modern, high-technology economy. This does not necessarily condemn them. Rapid economic growth is not to be taken as 'the chief end of man'. It cannot be considered irrational for the British to choose to sacrifice such growth to other purposes, *viz.* the preservation of cherished institutions and ways of life. That charge could only be laid against them if they were to demand both the fruits of rapid growth and the preservation of institutions that are inconsistent with it. Not that all the qualities of life for which the British have shown regard, such as good fellowship and 'economic chivalry' even in business relationships, are incompatible with efficiency. Some of the popular esteem for small enterprises is attributable to their providing a more genial environment for the flowering of such qualities than the great concerns, without any necessary detriment to efficiency. But it is one of the main themes of this *Paper* that other strongly-rooted institutions and attitudes are hostile to economic progress in the modern world. If the British are determined to cling to them, then they must be ready to accommodate their aspirations towards material progress to the mediocrity of their economic performance.

British reluctance to learn from others

It might have been expected that the economic achievements of other countries in recent decades would have aroused the curiosity of the British about the reasons for their success. Unfortunately, foreign example, whether in education or in political and industrial affairs, does not commend itself to the British, who have not shown themselves apt or willing pupils of those to whom they now concede the palm. They still act and speak as if all solutions must have a domestic origin and as if foreigners have little to teach them. It is true that attention is occasionally called to foreign models. At the very beginning of the present century an enterprising Lancastrian took a team of trade unionists to the United States so that they might observe American methods of manufacture.[88] Just after the Second World War groups of manufacturers and workers again went to America under the Anglo-American Productivity Scheme. Lately, a group of trade unionists from the iron and steel industry was given an opportunity of examining the highly efficient Japanese steel plants. In the course of official inquiries into industries the members of the investigating body have often been taken to countries where the corresponding industry is supposed to be well conducted.

But the industrial tourists, while admiring the methods of their foreign hosts, usually, on their return, bend their minds to finding reasons why foreign ways would not succeed here. The executives of the big international concerns appreciate the force of foreign example, but the lessons have little effect on conduct over the mass of the industry. The roots of this complacency go very deep. Even in the 16th century an Englishman who wished to pay a foreigner a compliment could think of no higher tribute than to tell him that he might be taken for an Englishman. Present attitudes are almost identical to those of a century ago when Matthew Arnold spoke of the 'exuberant self-satisfaction of the British'. Their general attitude, he said, could be summed up in such words as : 'Don't let us trouble ourselves about foreign thought; we shall invent the whole thing for ourselves as we go along.'[89]

Recently, a former General Secretary of the TUC brushed aside a foreign critic of British industrial relations by the condescending remark : 'We are a very funny people—difficult for foreigners to understand.' He had his counterpart in the Member of Parliament who said to Arnold : 'That a thing is an anomaly, I consider to be no objection to it whatever.'[90]

[88] This was the Moseley Industrial Commission to the United States of America (1902).
[89] Matthew Arnold, 'The Function of Criticism at the Present Time', *National Review*, November 1864, reprinted in *Essays Literary and Critical* (Everyman Edition), pp. 14, 18.
[90] *Ibid.*, p. 8.

VI. THE SOLUTION: DEEP-SEATED ADAPTATION TO INDUSTRIAL SOCIETY

If my diagnosis is correct, the 'British Disease' will not be cured by any of the remedies commonly prescribed for it, although they may relieve its symptoms. Its origin is not to be sought simply in the mistakes in economic policy since the war (such as the alleged mismanagement of demand, excessive government expenditure, inept decisions about investment), except in so far as these have arisen out of a deep-seated malady. The same is true of Britain's labour troubles. The contention is that the main fault resides in the failure of British institutions and attitudes of mind to adapt themselves to the requirements of a high-technology, industrial society. Those institutions and attitudes were once well-fitted to the tasks that confronted the nation at the time they came into being, and they formed a solid foundation for its success. But they remained entrenched at a period when the world was on the march, with disastrous consequences for the country's prosperity.

Resistance to change compounded by social structure

The debilitating effects of this resistance to change have been sketched. For many years past the successful management of economic affairs has called for the services of trained professionals. But Britain retained her love of the amateur, an inheritance from an aristocratic society by its bourgeois successors. Her class system, fortified by a divisive educational system, became increasingly incompatible with social harmony and economic efficiency as more and more of the industrial workers ceased to find the unqualified exercise of managerial authority acceptable.

The values cultivated by, or associated with, the country's social and educational institutions led to a diversion of first-rate, trained ability from industry and trade and to a neglect, for many years, of science, technology and vocational studies. The schools and universities turned out a number of very able and devoted civil servants, highly skilled in handling the problems of imperial administration and parliamentary procedures, but they failed to equip men with the expertise and judgement needed for taking decisions on the complicated industrial questions that arose as the government sector expanded and as technology became more elaborate.

Because Britain was fortunate enough to have avoided a major national calamity or revolution, those in control of affairs remained at the helm long after they had passed their prime, and they chose successors cut to the same pattern as themselves. For this reason old ways and men of the old type[91] continued to prevail in Britain long after their counterparts had been replaced in other countries. The infirmity of purpose that has disfigured British policy since the war may be traced, in some part, to that source; it presented a striking contrast to the concentrated resolve of the states that have enjoyed the most success. In industry Britain, like other nations, needed to make a fresh start after the war, but, through defects in her leadership, she often wasted her strength in efforts to sustain the structural *status quo.*

Recovery long and painful: a change in values and institutions

The process of recovery is likely to be long and perhaps painful. The fundamental problems of Britain are not such as will yield to a purely intellectual solution. Keynes is said to have told Churchill during the war that 'the post-war problems would be quite soluble with a little wise management'.[92] But wise management, if the present author is right, is conditional upon a shift in values and the transformation of institutions. One cannot expect quick results. The Dark Tower will not fall at the blast of a Childe Roland's slug-horn, however valiant he may be. The changes have to be made gradually and piecemeal if we are to avoid disorder : 'With time and patience the mulberry leaf becomes satin.' But sufficient time may not be granted to us, and patience is now a scarce commodity.

VII. THE WAY FORWARD

This diagnosis of the 'British Disease' must raise the question of curative treatment. It is clearly impossible to lay down any programme of reform, since the whole purport of the *Paper* is that remedies are to be sought in changes in institutions and attitudes, and these are not to be accomplished simply by Acts of Parliament or new administrative devices. Detailed remedial measures

91 *Moribus antiquis stat res Romana virisque!*
92 R. F. Harrod, *The Life of John Maynard Keynes*, Macmillan, 1951, p. 471.

must follow, not precede, the changes; and widespread recognition of the truth of the diagnosis should itself have an effect in altering attitudes and modifying institutions. But it is reasonable to ask, in addition, what steps can be taken to encourage the desired changes and to foster the attitudes consonant with a progressive society. The suggestions put forward below are necessarily of a broad character; if any readers intimately associated with industry, government and the trade unions accept the general sense of the diagnosis they, and they alone, would be competent to convert generalities into instruments of reform. But the broad lines of treatment seem evident enough, and some suggestions are set out below.

Reward the successful

1. If the British really wish to restore industrial prosperity to their country and to raise their standard of living, they must be ready to change their order of priorities. Policy must be directed to the encouragement of those whose aptitude lies in promoting industrial and commercial enterprise. The community must not grudge ample rewards for the successful, and the exercise of high business talent must not be frustrated. Unless the present frustrations are removed, industry will fail, as in the past, to attract a sufficiently large proportion of the country's most able men and women. It is only countries that aim at, and achieve, a high rate of growth that can afford lavish provisions for welfare and amenity.

Stop subsidies to the unsuccessful

2. Governments must abandon their predilection for supporting the *status quo* in economic life, for curbing the innovators because they disturb entrenched interests. Governments that allow themselves to fall under the influence of powerful sectional interests with a restrictionist outlook (e.g. trade unions) are dubious allies of the change inseparable from economic progress. Economic progress is not compatible with the disbursement of massive subsidies to support industries that cannot hold their own in a competitive environment.

Higher priority for economic growth to support other aims

3. It is not the contention of this *Paper* that economic growth should be 'the chief end of man', but only that, recently, economic growth has been assigned such a low place on Britain's

scale of preferences as to make impossible the attainment of other ends by which she sets great store.

Relate privileges and rewards to achievement, not status

4. One of the major obstacles in the path of Britain's economic progress is to be found in the divisiveness of British society, the existence of the 'two nations', a condition strengthened by the growing influence of Marxist doctrines. This is incompatible with the fruitful co-operation of men of all classes in the pursuit of a common purpose. It has been suggested that the fault lies, in large measure, in the transmission of attitudes fostered by the hierarchical society of the past into the modern world. An example of the expression of this social cleavage in industry is shown in the division between staff and shop-floor workers, and in the privileges given to the former. In this respect British practice can be contrasted with that prevailing in a number of progressive societies. Differences in privileges, as in rewards, should be related to function and achievement rather than status, which embodies the social attitudes of the past. This is being increasingly recognised in British industry, but there are many unregenerate sectors.[93] The old attitudes are still found at many levels in society and it is to be deplored that trade union militants do much to keep them alive and so to impede progress towards harmony. Representative bodies in industry, and educational institutions where entrants into industry are trained, could do much to encourage new attitudes.

Raise standards of state primary schools to improve opportunities for intellect and character

5. It has been suggested that the divisive educational system (a system peculiar to Britain) has contributed to the continuance of attitudes and social relations hostile to a modern, efficient economy. Every country's educational system must provide for the training of an élite, but this must be selected on grounds of intellect and character rather than social standing if class conflicts are not to be exacerbated. The absence of a common system of primary education must bear much of the blame and here foreign example is to be commended. A satisfactory remedy

[93] In an article in *The Times* (Business News, 9 March, 1976) Eric Wigham writes of this disparate treatment of staff and manual workers which exemplifies the 'class divisions in our society which so often astonish foreign visitors'. The British Institute of Management has deplored 'the artificial and divisive barriers which result from the concept of the "two sides" of industry'.

cannot be found by way of compulsion, and parental choice should not be fettered. Perhaps one must be content with hopes for a gradual erosion of older social attitudes and a continuous improvement in the standards of the state primary schools.

More civil servants should be educated in science and technology

6. It is argued that the Civil Service, admirable in the discharge of its traditional functions, has shown itself inept in handling the technological and economic problems of a science-based society in which the state plays a leading role in directing industrial development. The intelligent amateur still has a function to perform in government as in other walks of life, but a much larger number of civil servants than at present should be recruited from among those with an education relevant to the work they have to do, especially scientists and technologists. The professional in government and in industry has too often been denied the influence on decision-making that he deserves.

There should be a retreat from economic centralisation and new rules for operating the public sector

7. Government, to judge by the record of the last 25 years, has frequently shown itself at fault in dealing with the wide range of complicated technological and economic issues that have arisen through its increased participation in the economy. In large degree the fault can be ascribed simply to the very extension of its economic role, to the increased centralisation of decision-making that inevitably results, and to the absence in the public sector of the discipline that competition imposes. But some of the blame rests with the training of those who have to make the decisions and with the legal and administrative arrangements for which Parliament is ultimately responsible. For instance, some defects in the running of the nationalised industries can be ascribed to the lack of a clear definition of the respective powers of Ministers and Boards; the confusion and ambiguity that at present exist should be removed.[94]

More professional training for management necessary

8. There are limits to the contribution of the academy to the training of business men. The untaught business genius will always make his mark in a liberal society. But even he, if he is

[94] Sir Norman Chester, *The Nationalisation of British Industry, 1945–51*, HMSO, 1975, especially Chap. XI.

to fulfil himself, must be served by highly trained professionals, and the supply of these people must depend to a considerable extent on a specialised education, such as that provided by Schools of Business Studies.

More attention to industrial relations by managements

9. Recent experience indicates that the law has only a modest part to play in the reform of Britain's troubled industrial relations. The evolution of a more rational trade union structure must come from impulse within the movement, but government and management can at least lend support to those trade union leaders who are trying to put things right. Good industrial relations are, in large part, the result of wise and skilled management, and firms which give high priority to these relations and where a senior director is placed in charge of them, are likely to have a better record in this respect than those who concern themselves with industrial relations only when trouble arises. The monopolistic powers of trade unions exert their maximum influence in industries which are themselves insulated by restrictive trading practices, monopoly, or tariffs and other forms of government protection, from the discipline of a competitive market.

Leave scope for diversity in industrial organisation

10. Policy on industrial organisation has been much affected by fashion and has tended to follow opinion which oscillates between favouring, at one time large concerns and consolidations, at another small firms. Here there should be no general rule. An efficient economy leaves scope for diversity. At present the scale is weighted against the small family business. Yet these, for all their defects, display social and economic merits which the community should value. Small firms have been a fertile source of innovations in the past and, in general, industrial relations in such firms have been more harmonious than in very large establishments. It is true that many family businesses have been unprogressive and some of them have from time to time been burdened by the obligation to find jobs for incompetent relatives, but, in the highly competitive and progressive economy which it should be government's aim to establish, such businesses would have short shrift.

POSTSCRIPT

TO THE SECOND EDITION

Britain on the wrong economic road

In the three years that have elapsed since the First Edition of this *Paper* was written, the 'British Disease' has tightened its grip on the body politic. The diagnosis presented in the *Paper* has been widely accepted, but little attempt has been made to apply remedies. In fact, one of the causes of the trouble, the discouragement of enterprise by various acts of government and by institutions hostile to economic efficiency, has become more manifest than ever. The last three years have, however, brought with them one significant change. In the original text, the complacency of the British, as evinced in their repudiation of foreign example or prescription, was the subject of remark. This attitude has not been sustained. The British can no longer make light of their deficiencies. Their mood has become chastened and humble.

As yet, however, the loss of self-esteem does not seem to have been accompanied by any national resolve to redeem the errors of the past. Nor has it induced any general recognition that the fulfilment of what are held to be reasonable expectations in regard to income and welfare depends on economic performance. Indeed, to judge from the industrial disorders of the early months of 1979, its main consequence has been to turn conflicts between social classes into bitter struggles among rival functional or occupational groups. Meanwhile, the relative position of Britain in the world economy has continued to deteriorate. The Table on page 78 sets out comparative performances during the last few years.

Olson's 'stage of development' explanation

Before presenting some additional evidence and argument in support of the main thesis of the *Paper*, I must comment on a proposition that has been put forward by an American economist, Professor Mancur Olson, and has found favour with Mr Samuel Brittan. The proposition, by no means novel, is that the disease from which Britain is suffering is not peculiar to her but is associated with the stage in economic and political development that she has reached.

Table 1

COMPARATIVE ECONOMIC PERFORMANCE:
1973 and 1977
(1970 = 100)

	GNP		Industrial Production		Output per Man-hour	
	1973	*1977*	*1973*	*1977*	*1973*	*1977*
UK	111	111	111	106	118	121
USA	118	124	120	127	113	127
West Germany	112	119	113	116	117	139
France	113	131	120	126	121	139
Japan	129	145	127	127	133	155

'The longer the period in which a country has had a modern industrial pattern of common interest and at the same time freedom of organisation without upheavals and disruption, the greater the extent to which its growth rate will be retarded by organised interests.'[1]

Britain pioneered the industrial revolution and has had a long experience of freedom and settled institutions, whereas most of the other developed countries came to industrialism later and their political evolution has been disturbed by periods of instability. As Toynbee might have said, they have had to gird themselves at intervals to meet challenges to their survival.

Up to a point, this proposition is in line with some of the explanations for Britain's troubles that have been advanced in this *Paper*. On page 65 it is argued that the absence of any sharp break in her political evolution meant that institutions and attitudes called into being by the needs of times past were preserved long after they had served their purpose. In the end she found herself in an institutional *impasse* from which she has as yet failed to discover an exit.

To recognise the significance of Britain's historical legacy, however, is by no means to admit that the course she has followed is one that all must take, still less that it is one from which she cannot break away. Neither experience nor reason

[1] M. Olson, *The Logic of Collective Action*, Harvard University Press, Cambridge, Mass., 2nd Edition, 1971, and S. Brittan, *How English is the English Sickness?*, Henry Simons Lecture, delivered at the University of Chicago Law School, 4 April 1978.

provides a warrant for such a determinist view of a country's fate. On pages 64-5 I set out my reasons for repudiating the theory, of convergent social evolution favoured alike by Marx, Galbraith and, at times, Schumpeter. A nation's future is settled by its choices. Although mistaken choices at critical moments in its history may predispose it towards a succession of such mistakes, they do not eliminate its freedom of decision. The increasing complexity of society and technology may, for instance, give rise to the problem of reconciling collective demands with the operation of a market economy, and may lead all advanced countries to extend the functions of the State. Yet, the way these functions are exercised and their impact on economic progress depend on the nature of the national purpose. Where State intervention is directed towards promoting economic efficiency or towards improving the functioning of the market, the consequences for the country's material progress will be very different from where efficiency is assigned a low place in the government's scale of preferences, or where the intervention operates against market forces. Public enterprise itself will wear a different complexion in a country where nationalisation has been determined by considerations of administrative convenience or expediency from that in a country where industries have been nationalised in obedience to a political doctrine or a social theory.

Again, the much admired German and Japanese systems of industrial relations, which emerged out of the confusions of the post-war years, may work less smoothly than hitherto if, as is likely, the rate of industrial growth in those countries declines. But there is no reason to suppose that the Germans and the Japanese are condemned to model their industrial relations in the future on the British system, which is the product of a unique social and political experience. Indeed, it is more likely that Britain's industrial relations will provide a cautionary guide for the whole world.

The deficiencies of the British educational system

Let us consider another aspect of this question of inevitable fate. It is suggested in the original text of this *Paper* that an important cause of Britain's failure to adjust her economy to the age of high technology can be traced to blemishes in her educational system. Until recently, British education, in some of its branches, might well recall to its critics the reproach of Francis Bacon when he spoke of an 'infinite agitation of wit' which produced 'cobwebs of learning admirable for the fineness of the thread and work, but of no substance or profit'.[1] Throughout the whole system disdain for vocational training and laggardliness in developing scientific and technical education were among the chief faults. Technologists ranked low in public esteem, and both they and scientists are even today allowed to exert only a modest influence on policy-making in government and industry.

These deficiencies are widely recognised. Several committees of inquiry, both official and private, have proclaimed them, and more will be said presently about their consequences for industrial management.[2] Here we will simply point the contrast with European countries in this respect. In Germany the social prestige of the *Gymnasium*, with its strongly classical bias, did not prevent the emergence of a first-class system of technical education. As the historian of ICI has pointed out, it would have been impossible for Ludwig Mond to have found in England the opportunities for scientific and technical education that prepared him for his career as an innovator in the British chemical industry.[3] French education also was much involved in traditional classical studies. Nevertheless, among the Grandes Écoles, the École Polytechnique and other schools of high professional and technical training enjoyed parity of esteem with the École Normale Supérieure. From these institutions there has proceeded a flow of graduates well equipped to handle the problems of modern industry, an élite to whom France owes much of her striking economic achievement of the last twenty years.

Trend to technology reversed by 1902 Education Act

Now the contrast with Britain cannot be ascribed solely to the prejudices of the old Universities and the public schools but can in part be traced to a number of unfortunate decisions

[1] Francis Bacon, *The Two Books of Francis Bacon of the Proficience and Advancement of Learning*, ed, W. A. Wright, Oxford, 1868, III, pp. 285-6.
[2] Department of Industry, *Industry, education and management*, July 1977; Production Management Action Group, *The Mismanagement of Production in the UK*, Administrative Staff College, Henley, June 1976; C. L. Bore, *On the Role, Status and Education of Engineers in British Industry*, Evidence submitted to the Committee of Inquiry into the Engineering Profession, 1978.
[3] W. J. Reader, *Imperial Chemical Industries: A History*, O.U.P., 1970, Vol. 1, p. 38.

taken at the beginning of the century. The Act of 1889, which gave the County Councils power to raise a rate for technical education, remained unfruitful until it was fertilised by the 'whisky money'.[1] It was this that 'really got technical education moving', and during the 1890s scientific and technical studies enjoyed such a boom that, in 1897, it was said that 'science is positively jostling other subjects out of the field'.[2] But the triumph was short-lived. Sir Robert Morant, who directed the great educational changes of the time, reversed the trend towards science and technology by moulding the new system of state secondary education on traditional lines. On this showing the Education Act of 1902, and the reconstructed Board of Education under Morant, had a deleterious effect on Britain's industrial future. Thus one may conclude that the fate of nations is not a function of the stage of development they have reached, but is determined by the decisions that their leaders choose to make and by the institutions they decide to set up. This proposition has been expounded at some length because the Olson thesis, if it were to have any practical influence, could only lead to despair. Britain *may* be persuaded to change her course; she is not doomed to remain the victim of her past errors.

The depreciation of science and technology

On pages 48-50 it was argued that Britain's relatively poor performance in several of the technologically advanced industries was in part attributable to the absence of applied scientists and technologists in sufficient force on the directing boards of companies. Evidence in support of this view has accumulated; Britain's lack of well-trained production managers has also been stressed. A quotation from a recent official report is relevant to these criticisms of British management:

---

[1] It is a measure of the indifference of government and parliament to technical education that the first public provision of money for it arose out of a fiscal accident. In 1890 a Bill was introduced to eliminate surplus public houses and a new duty on beer and spirits was imposed to pay compensation to the publicans. The plan failed, but as the money had already been voted, it was agreed, on the motion of an MP who was keen on technical education, that the money should go to the County Councils for that purpose. (M. Gowing, 'Science, Technology and Education: England in 1870', in the *Oxford Review of Education*, Vol. 4, No. 1, 1978, pp. 7-8; and R. C. K. Ensor, *England, 1870-1914*, O.U.P., 1936, p. 204n.)

[2] M. Gowing, *loc. cit.*, p. 8.

'. . . in manufacturing industry generally the status of mechanical engineering is low in itself, and production engineers are regarded as the Cinderella of the profession.'[1]

Qualified engineers and scientists have generally been recruited for their technical expertise rather than as potential top executives, as is the case on the Continent.[2]

No doubt the bias of the educational system described here is partly responsible, but a more satisfactory explanation is that British education and British management have been caught in a vicious circle. Because the status of engineers and technologists in business is low, and because their opportunities of reaching top executive positions are narrowly limited, the engineering departments at the Universities are unable to attract a high proportion of first-class students. The best of them, moreover, are inclined to seek careers in research rather than in production management (page 56). One consequence is that, in many firms, top management, because of the absence of technically-trained people among the directors, is liable to take decisions in ignorance of the production problems involved. Production managers for their part often lack the capacity or the opportunity to make clear to the directorate the complexity of the production tasks that result from the major decisions of policy.[3]

The contrast with the Continent is striking. In Germany production engineers enjoy a high social standing and are usually well-educated men. In France the engineers form the most heavily represented group in top management; and nine out of ten in a sample of chief executives were found to have had a university training. In Sweden the typical entrant into manufacturing industry is an engineering graduate who usually begins his career in a production department.[4]

The errors of government intervention

Something more must be said about the effect of government policy on Britain's performance. As was shown on pages 17-18, for many years after the Second World War the government relied on macro-economic measures of control and guidance. Even by the late 1950s, however, Britain's failure to keep pace with the rate of development of other countries had begun to

---

[1] Department of Industry, *op. cit.*, p. 31.
[2] Production Management Action Group, pp. 7-8.
[3] *Ibid.*, pp. 7-8.
[4] *Ibid.*

shake the faith of politicians in macro-economic measures. So the government set out to influence the economy by particular acts of intervention in business decisions. It brought about the reorganisation of several large industries (cotton, motor-cars, electrical engineering and shipbuilding, for example). The lavish subsidies given to support unprofitable firms and industries, and to coerce firms to locate their plants in officially favoured regions, have already been mentioned (pp. 23, 29). The government introduced measures designed to improve technical skills, to stimulate particular forms of investment, and to promote new systems of industrial administration, as in workers' co-operatives. If it failed to proceed with the recommendations of the Bullock Committee about industrial democracy (which in this instance meant simply the participation of the trade union bureaucracy in management), the reason was simply that the proposals were opposed both by the workers and the employers.

Government actions have borne little relation to its statements of intent. The Treasury and the Department of Industry committed themselves to the bold declaration that 'the broad thrust of the government's selective assistance policy is to invest in success'.[1] In fact, particular acts of intervention (especially when they took the form of providing State subsidies) were often governed by a desire to maintain the status quo, at any rate when employment was threatened, rather than by a concern with efficiency. For instance, financial help was given to the ailing Chrysler UK, despite the advice of the Industrial Development Advisory Board that the project offered no prospect of 'viability', advice that time has proved to be right. Some of the means designed to revivify manufacturing industry exerted an influence on the economy that was exactly opposite to that required. It had long been recognised that British industry suffered from over-manning. Yet the Selective Employment Tax, introduced in 1966, actually provided for subsidising employment in manufacturing industry at the expense of a poll tax on employment in other sectors.

One of the most ironical examples of government planning is to be seen in the effect on London of the location of industry policy. The policy of steering industry away from London in the interest of employment in the development areas was applied,

[1] Quoted in P. Mottershead, 'Industrial Policy', in F. T. Blackaby (ed.), *British Economic Policy, 1960-74*, Cambridge University Press, 1978, p. 481.

in 1965, to white-collar workers by the Control of Offices and Industrial Development Act. Ten years later London was found to be short of jobs and the policy was put into reverse. The authorities have lately been engaged in directing firms *into* London instead of *away* from it.

The government has enjoyed as little success when it has tried to foster new industries or products as when it has been propping up the old.

> 'The creation of a single computer company (International Computers) has resulted in persistent claims on government funds rather than a company capable of holding its own in world markets'.[1]

Other examples are given on page 22. An economist summed up his penetrating survey of industrial policy by stating that 'increased intervention has ... made little contribution to improving our economic performance'.[2] Was he not over-generous in his assessment?

The failure of government enterprise

In the State-owned sector the consequences of maladministration have become more obvious since this *Paper* was first written. Herbert Morrison, the architect of the post-war nationalisation, believed that the public corporation would inherit the best of all worlds. It would confer on the nation the benefits of vigorous industrial enterprise unimpeded by bureaucratic control together with those of public accountability. In practice, despite the lip-service paid by successive governments to the 'commercial principle' in the administration of national undertakings, efficiency has been frequently undermined by government interference in their price, wages and investment policies, usually in the pursuit of some political objective.[3] At one time (1972-74) the prices of the products or services of the nationalised undertakings were frozen, as an anti-inflation device, and the consequent losses were covered by subsidies. Later the Boards in control were required to hit financial targets, without subsidies, and so were compelled to raise their prices very steeply. Rational decision-making by management in the public and private sector

[1] *Ibid.*, p. 480.
[2] *Ibid.*, p. 482.
[3] S. C. Littlechild, *The Fallacy of the Mixed Economy*, Hobart Paper 80, IEA, 1978.

[84]

alike is made very difficult by such sudden and frequent changes in government policy and must certainly have affected the efficiency of administration.

The mischievous consequences of the government's interference in the location of new plants in the motor industry have already been referred to (page 29). But they were not isolated examples. One of the most conspicuous follies can be laid at the door of Mr Harold Macmillan when he was Prime Minister. In 1958 a decision was required about the siting of a new, massive steel strip mill. The Prime Minister, yielding to political pressure, decided that his government, instead of authorising the capital for one efficient mill, should finance *two* sub-optimal mills, one in Scotland and the other in South Wales.[1] He even claimed the wisdom of Solomon in his choice.

His Labour successors later frustrated the efforts of the British Steel Corporation to create an industry capable of holding its own in international competition by insisting, in response to the demands of the interested trade unions, that old, high-cost units should be kept in operation. The disastrous consequences of ignoring considerations of cost are patent, but government policy has ignored this evidence. In recent years the stated preferences of the electricity generating industry in regard to fuel have been set at nought in deference to the government's commitments to the coal industry. The latest example of this disposition to ignore the criteria of economic rationality is to be seen in the government's handling of the finances of the BBC. Instead of allowing the corporation to cover its costs by raising its licence fees (or by some method of charging) it has ordained that the money should be raised by additional borrowing : in effect, by a State subsidy.

One of the most dismal failures of public enterprise within recent years is to be found in housing. During the 1950s and 1960s planners, architects, development companies, politicians and civil servants (central and local) came together in a malign combination for the erection, at vast public expense, of numerous high-rise blocks of flats to which the local authorities have consigned multitudes of their unfortunate citizens. Some of these buildings have proved to be either so structurally unsound or so

---

[1] Peter Maunder, 'Government Intervention in the Economy of the United Kingdom', in Peter Maunder (ed.), *Government Intervention in the Developed Economy*, Groom Helm, 1979, for an admirable survey of this subject.

intolerable as dwelling places that they are now being pulled down, again at vast public expense. Contrast this lamentable experience with the history of housing in the 1930s. In that decade the speculative builder, derided and despised immediately after the war by the school of advanced social thinkers then in fashion, was able to provide millions of people with houses of the sort they liked at £400-450 apiece.[1]

The hamstringing of management

A final word may be said about industrial relations. The governments of both Sir Harold Wilson and Mr Edward Heath realised that, if anarchy in industrial relations was to be avoided, it was necessary to remove some of the legal privileges accorded to trade unions. But both governments lost their nerve in the face of trade union opposition and their efforts to ensure that industrial relations were governed by equal laws were abandoned. Since 1974 the government has taken an opposite course, in an attempt to induce the trade unions to fall in with its economic policies. A number of Acts have been passed which give the organised workers additional privileges and strengthen their bargaining power *vis-à-vis* their employers.[2] They have had the effect of reducing the ability of management in both the public and the private sector to maintain discipline, without doing anything to promote 'industrial democracy' or to involve workers in responsibility for business policy. These changes have been all the more damaging to the nation's economic health because of the tendency for power within the trade unions to shift from the central bureaucracy to the shop floor. In the early months of 1979 the price of these follies was being paid by the British public.

[1] 'In 20 [interwar] years, four million houses were built, 1.1 million by local authorities and 2.9 million by private enterprise, 400,000 of which were subsidised. By the outbreak of the second world war, one-third of the country's dwelling stock was new. The building industry delivered the remarkable total of 1.6 million dwellings in the boom period, 1935-1939.' (Gordon Cherry, 'Homes for heroes; semis for bypasses', *New Society*, 1 February 1979.)

[2] The Acts include the Trade Union and Labour Relations Act of 1974 which abolished the National Industrial Relations Court set up by the previous government; the Trade Union and Labour Relations (Amendment) Act of 1976 which virtually conceded the principle of the 'closed shop'; the Employment Protection Act of 1975 which considerably strengthened the employees' bargaining power and turned the formerly independent Advisory, Conciliation and Arbitration Service (ACAS) into a statutory body; the Redundancy Payments Act of 1975; and several others. Whatever their merits, these laws all added to the burden of bureaucratic overheads that industry had to bear and made the tasks of already sorely tried managements more difficult.

[86]

A few years ago a distinguished economist argued that Britain's chief difficulties were the result simply of temporary disorders which could easily be cured. Britain, as she put it, had got herself into an 'awkward corner'.[1] An Awkward Corner? It is the contention of this *Paper* that for many years our country has been travelling on the wrong road.

February 1979   G. C. ALLEN

[1] Joan Robinson, *An Awkward Corner*, Allen and Unwin, 1966.

QUESTIONS FOR DISCUSSION

1. How far are the faster rates of economic advance in the USA, Europe and more recently Japan than in Britain due to differences in the degree of competition, in institutions that welcomed or resisted change, and in general attitudes to achievement in industry contrasted with the professions?

2. Does the structure of British society bear any responsibility for the mediocre performance of Britain compared with that of other countries in recent decades? In what respects, if any, is Britain peculiar?

3. What part can academic training play in equipping men to manage industrial concerns?

4. Why have industrialists and business men in general fallen in esteem in Britain in the present century? Compare their status in Britain with that in other countries.

5. To what extent can we learn from foreign example in education, business organisation, public administration and industrial relations?

6. What are the respective merits of the amateur and the expert in business or official life?

7. Why are firms sometimes reluctant to use differential salary scales to allocate trained personnel to suit their requirements?

8. Have British trade unions been more obstructive to innovation than their foreign counterparts? If so, why?

9. Have restrictive practices by industrialists and traders been responsible for retarding growth and necessary adaptations in British industry?

10. Since Britain's national income has risen at a faster rate since 1950 than in the earlier years of the century, how do you explain the dissatisfaction with the country's economic performance?

NOTE ON READING

The books and articles referred to in footnotes to the text should be useful for further reading. R. E. Caves and Associates, *Britain's Economic Prospects* (Allen & Unwin, 1968) and Sir Alec Cairncross (ed.), *Britain's Economic Prospects Reconsidered* (Allen & Unwin, 1971) present a searching analysis by distinguished economists, British and American, of the causes of Britain's relatively low rate of growth since the war. W. H. B. Court, *British Economic History, 1870–1914* (CUP, 1965) contains a most useful collection of documents and much illuminating comment on British economic development before the First World War. Alfred Marshall, *Industry and Trade* (Macmillan, 1921), W. J. Ashley's *The Tariff Problem* (King, 2nd edn., 1904), B. Bowker, *Lancashire Under the Hammer* (L. & V. Woolf, 1928), P. H. Hohenberg, *Chemicals in Western Europe, 1850–1914* (North-Holland, 1967) discuss, at different levels of scholarship, British industrial problems in the years before 1914. D. L. Burns, *The Economic History of Steelmaking, 1867–1939* (CUP, 1940) is an authoritative work of great value in assessing Britain's economic performance. C. Erickson, *British Industrialists, Steel and Hosiery 1850–1950* (CUP, 1959) is a detailed case study of the origins and character of industrial leaders in two contrasted types of industry.

There are many studies of British economic development in the present century that have a bearing on the theme of this essay, including A. J. Youngson, *The British Economy 1920–57* (Allen & Unwin, 1960), S. Pollard, *The Development of the British Economy 1914–1950* (Arnold, 1962), and even G. C. Allen's *The Structure of Industry in Britain: A Study in Economic Change* (Longmans, 3rd edn., 1970). Structural adaptation in British industry is examined in W. E. G. Salter, *Productivity and Technical Change* (CUP, 2nd edn., 1966), and the process in a particular area in G. C. Allen, *The Industrial Development of Birmingham and the Black Country, 1860–1927* (Frank Cass, 1929, reprinted 1965).

Industrial innovation is examined in a series of studies undertaken at University College, London, *viz.* M. Bowley, *Innovations in Building Materials* (1960), W. J. Corlett, *The Economic Development of Detergents* (1958), A. G. Donnithorne, *British Rubber Manufacturing* (1958), D. C. Hague, *The Economics of Man-Made Fibres* (1957), S. G. Sturmey, *The Economic*

Development of Radio (1958), and M. Wray, *The Women's Outerwear Industry* (1957); all these were published by Duckworth. Science, technology and education in science in the period covered by this essay are examined in D. S. L. Cardwell, *The Organisation of Science in England* (Heinemann, rev. edn., 1972). C. F. Carter and B. R. Williams, *Scientists in Industry* (OUP, 1959) is also very useful. The state of education for business in various countries during the early part of this century is reviewed in W. J. Ashley, *Commercial Education* (Williams & Norgate, 1926). J. Jewkes, D. Sawers and S. Stillerman, *The Sources of Invention* (Macmillan, 2nd edn., 1969) is full of information and shrewd comment on invention and innovation in industry.

There are many useful studies of industrial relations between which it is difficult to discriminate, but no-one interested in the subject should fail to read E. Phelps Brown, *The Trade Union and the Common Weal* (OUP, 1967). For a brilliant and concise comparative study of the major European economies, read M. M. Postan, *An Economic History of Western Europe, 1945–64* (Methuen, 1967); the chapters on 'Innovation', 'The Managers' and 'The Managed', are especially relevant to matters discussed in this *Paper*. For the Japanese way of handling problems of management and industrial relations there are R. Dore, *British Factory—Japanese Factory* (Allen & Unwin, 1973), and J. Hirschmeier and T. Yui, *The Development of Japanese Business, 1600–1973* (Allen & Unwin, 1975).

Press Comments on the First Edition

Why Britain is in the doldrums

'English public schools and the university bias against vocational education are partly to blame for Britain's industrial and economic malaise.

... Professor G. C. Allen ... accuses public schools of failing to provide leaders who can manage Britain's economy in general and industry in particular.'

Times Educational Supplement

Reward could stop UK rot

'Out-of-date ways and old-fashioned men are blamed for Britain's economic ills in a new study by Professor G. C. Allen.

Mistakes in post-war economic policy, such as excessive Government spending and wrong decisions on investment, are not the simple explanation of what went wrong, Professor Allen says ... He believes the main fault lay in our failure to adapt our institutions and attitudes to the demands of the modern, high-technology industrial society.'

Guardian

The snobbish truth about Britain's road to ruin

'... I am obliged to the Institute of Economic Affairs, in these straw-clutching times, for providing a straw to clutch at.

Our trouble, according to the Institute, is that we are too stupid.

Well, not exactly. What the pamphlet "The British Disease" says is that fewer smart people in this country are engaged in industry than in similar countries like France, Germany or Japan.

Our trouble is snobbery, more than anything else.

The author of this depressive, Professor Allen, diagnoses the British Disease somewhat differently to those people who put it down to idleness, complacency or strikes. He thinks we are not clever enough.

And he explains why. Our best brains, mainly for snobbish reasons, go into the civil service and the professions instead of manufacturing industry.

He put up a solid case for the view, leaden with footnotes, and what is especially nasty is that the chickens that are coming home to roost now in the headlines have been crackled-over for at least a century.'

Jon Akass, *Sun*

Britain's decline due to 'Outdated thinking'

'Professor Allen contrasts the mischievous effects of that snobbery on the steel industry with industries, such as glassmaking, confectionery and brewing where family businesses kept their vigour and still flourish.

Public schools turned out political leaders and administrators but failed to provide leaders equipped to manage Britain's economy and industry when her commercial supremacy was waning.

Universities did not make up for the schools' failure.'

Liverpool Daily Post

Industry suffers from another 'British disease'

'The British education system must provide for the training of an elite selected on the grounds of intellect and character rather than social standing, Professor G. C. Allen ... has warned in a new paper on the country's lagging economy ... he argues that the divisive educational system in Britain has contributed to the continuance of attitudes and social relations hostile to an efficient, modern working economy. He maintains that more civil servants should be recruited from among scientists, technologists and others with relevant education, and calls on industry to increase recruitment of highly trained professionals produced by the specialist business schools.

In comparison with other countries, industry in Britain has not attracted a high proportion of those with first rate ability. The inclination of the best graduates is still to prefer an academic career, research, the civil service or the professions to jobs in industry.'

Sue Reid, *The Times Higher Education Supplement*

IEA PUBLICATIONS

Subscription Service

An annual subscription is the most convenient way to obtain our publications. Every title we produce in all our regular series will be sent to you immediately on publication and without further charge, representing a substantial saving.

Subscription rates *

Britain: £15.00 p.a. including postage.

£14.00 p.a. if paid by Banker's Order.

£10.00 p.a. teachers and students who pay *personally.*

Europe and South America: 40 US dollars or equivalent.

Other countries: Rates on application. In most countries subscriptions are handled by local agents.

*These rates are *not* available to companies or to institutions.

To: The Treasurer, Institute of Economic Affairs,
2 Lord North Street,
Westminster, London SW1P 3LB.

I should like to subscribe beginning....................................
I enclose a cheque/postal order for:

☐ £15.00

☐ Please send me a Banker's Order form

☐ Please send me an Invoice

☐ £10.00 [I am a teacher/student at ....]

Name...

Address...

....

Signed.. Date.................

HP67/2